"Yes, Eva, I want it all. The chorizo, the ch[...] tequila. In *My Mexican Kitchen*, we get th[...] Eva Longoria and her quest to show off the gr[...] culinary history Mexico has to offer. I'll be feeding my friends and family with these recipes. First up, Pollo Asado!"

—**BOBBY FLAY**, chef and bestselling author

"Eva Longoria beautifully captures the essence of Mexican and Latin American experiences in this carefully curated collection of accessible recipes that celebrates the country's heritage. In her cookbook, she takes us beyond just tacos, revealing the diverse culinary world of Mexico, and pours authenticity, passion, and cultural richness into each story."

—**LORENA GARCIA**, celebrity chef, restaurateur, philanthropist, and author of *Lorena Garcia's New Taco Classics*

"Eva has a passion for food, authenticity, and storytelling like very few people I know. In *My Mexican Kitchen*, we all get to experience that magic and learn not only fabulous recipes but also how they can shape you as a person and cook."

—**MICHAEL SYMON**, James Beard Award–winning chef, restaurateur, Food Network host, and author of *Simply Symon Suppers*

"The remarkably varied deliciousness that blossoms daily from Mexico's regional kitchens easily captures hearts. That's what Eva Longoria discovered as she explored beyond the flavors of her Texas-Mexican roots to the fabled specialties of cities and pueblos from the Rio Grande to the azure Caribbean waters of the Yucatán. And in *My Mexican Kitchen*, she shares those culinary adventures in stories, history, and, of course, a collection of recipes that celebrates her travels and the vibrancy of her home kitchen. The honest flavors Eva shares will no doubt capture your heart, too."

—**RICK BAYLESS**, award-winning author, chef, and host of PBS's *Mexico: One Plate at a Time*

EVA LONGORIA

with *Thea Baumann*

MY MEXICAN KITCHEN

100 Recipes Rich with Tradition, Flavor, and Spice

Photographs by Matt Armendariz

CLARKSON POTTER/PUBLISHERS
NEW YORK

To all the amazing people I met while filming Searching for Mexico, *I will be forever grateful to you for showing me a Mexico I didn't know existed*

All rights reserved.
Published in the United States by Clarkson Potter/ Publishers, an imprint of the Crown Publishing Group, a division of Penguin Random House LLC, New York.
ClarksonPotter.com

CLARKSON POTTER is a trademark and POTTER with colophon is a registered trademark of Penguin Random House LLC.

Library of Congress Cataloging-in-Publication Data is available upon request.

ISBN 978-0-593-79642-9
Signed Edition ISBN 978-0-593-80052-2
Ebook ISBN 978-0-593-79643-6

Printed in China

Editor: Raquel Pelzel
Editorial assistant: Elaine Hennig
Designer: Mia Johnson
Production editor: Patricia Shaw
Production manager: Kim Tyner
Compositors: Merri Ann Morrell, Nick Patton
Food stylist: Adam C. Pearson
Food stylist assistants: Diana Kim, Elle Debell
Prop stylist: Abby Pendergrast
Prop stylist assistant: Kitty Rheault
Photo assistants: Wade Hammond, Joe Elgar
Digital techs: Justin Manzano, Tom Mishima
Copy editor: Kate Slate
Proofreaders: Sigi Nacson, Kim Lewis
Indexer: Elizabeth T. Parson
Publicists: David Hawk, Felix Cruz
Marketer: Stephanie Davis

10 9 8 7 6 5 4 3 2 1

First Edition

Contents

Introduction

I wrote my first cookbook thirteen years ago, and although I've cooked every day since it was published, I haven't felt like I had anything worthy of writing down again until now. My last book was a memoir of my life told through food. I was married to a Frenchman at the time and the recipes were a beautiful mix of new favorites influenced by my frequent stays in France, family recipes I learned from my aunt Elsa, friends' recipes, and more, all woven together with personal stories.

I so clearly remember telling my editor that, while I planned to include some Mexican dishes, I didn't want the book to be all Mexican food. I saw my cooking as a reflection of me and, although my Mexican heritage is an essential part of my identity, I didn't want to be defined solely by it.

Here we are, a decade later, and I split my time between Mexico City and Los Angeles, have a Mexican husband and son, and, after a life-changing trip through Mexico for my show on CNN, *Searching for Mexico*, I can't imagine writing a book about anything but Mexican food and how it relates to culture, traditions, and history—both of Mexico and my own.

I'm a thirteenth-generation American. My ancestors came into the port of Veracruz from Spain and settled on a ranch just north of the Rio Grande, in what was then Mexico but, after the Treaty of Hidalgo in the mid-nineteenth century, became Texas.

I grew up in Corpus Christi, Texas, on breakfast tacos, Aunt Elsa's tamales, and my dad's famous menudo—Mexican food and Tex-Mex food are definitely in my DNA. But, as I learned when I left south Texas, the version of Mexican cuisine I grew up with—flour tortillas, Frito pie, and smoky esquites from just across the border in Nuevo León—is not everyone's. I've always told people that Mexican food is so much more than tacos and tequila, but until I started traveling throughout the country, and especially after I married my husband, Pepe, and moved to Mexico City, I had no idea how multifaceted and diverse it really was.

When CNN approached me about *Searching for Mexico*, I couldn't say no. Four months traveling around this food mecca and eating all day? Don't threaten me with a good time! I expected to taste some great dishes and meet some wonderful people, but I never could have imagined just how impactful the experience would be. In those four months, we traveled coast to coast, north to south, eating some of the best food in the world and hearing the stories behind it. I'd been to several of Mexico's thirty-two states before, but for the show, we went to so many places I never would have found on my own. Like the home kitchen of three wonderfully sassy Muxes (the nonbinary Zapotec community in Oaxaca who identify as a third gender), chef Alberto Kuku's backyard píib (a traditional underground oven used throughout the Yucatán Peninsula) at his home in Xocén, and Lake Chapala in Jalisco, where I fished and cooked with the Coca people, one of the oldest indigenous groups in all of Mexico. I visited farmers, archaeologists, cowboys, chefs, and home cooks. I saw firsthand just how regional the food in this country is—cooking styles and recipes varied from state to state, town to town, and even household to household—and I was continually struck by the importance placed on ingredients.

If French food is rooted in technique, Mexican food is rooted in ingredients and history. It's a fascinating combination of ancient culinary traditions centered around plants endemic to Mesoamerica—like chocolate, vanilla, tomatoes, and beans—mixed with new ingredients and techniques introduced over centuries of colonization and immigration. I learned that Jewish immigrants escaping the Spanish Inquisition likely invented the flour tortilla, using flour brought from Spain to make an unleavened bread, and that tacos al pastor, which are cooked on the same type of spit used for shawarma, were developed by Turkish and Lebanese immigrants who came over in the nineteenth and early twentieth centuries. Standing at the port of Veracruz where my family, along with so many others, first entered the country unlocked something in me. It opened my eyes and showed me how vast, beautiful, and ever-changing Mexican cuisine really is: based on essential ingredients, shared traditions, and exciting new influences.

When I got back to the United States, I couldn't stop cooking. I was re-creating dishes I'd learned on the road and developing new ones using Mexican ingredients I now had a whole new appreciation for. The trip was a real full-circle moment. It reminded me that Mexican culture is, and will always be, deeply rooted in my identity and my food.

This cookbook is a celebration of that, as well as the endlessly knowledgeable cooks and teachers who have generously taught me over the years. It's the food I grew up eating, the recipes and stories shared by all the people I met on my travels, and the dishes I was inspired to create when I got home. They're full of history, love, flavor, and spice. I hope they change your life the same way they've changed mine.

XO,

ESSENTIAL PANTRY ITEMS, PRODUCE, and TOOLS

The pantry is the backbone of the kitchen. I think Martha Stewart has an entire book about a pantry! Mine isn't that extensive, but there are definitely some dry goods, fresh ingredients, and tools that I rely on to make all my Mexican recipes (and that you'll need in order to cook from this book). As long as my kitchen is stocked with these essentials, I know I can throw together something delicious with whatever else I have in the fridge. . . .

PANTRY

PILONCILLO SUGAR

Piloncillo is a form of raw cane sugar that comes densely packed in blocks, loaves, or cones (the shape is determined by the mold that the extracted and cooked sugar cane syrup is poured into) and keeps forever. It is similar in flavor to light brown sugar but is a little sweeter and a little more caramel-y. I use the small holes on a box grater to grate the piloncillo that I call for throughout the book. You can easily find it at any Latin market or online. If you don't have piloncillo, feel free to substitute light brown sugar.

MEXICAN VANILLA

Mexican vanilla beans and extract are a must in any Mexican pantry! Although it's endemic to Mexico, because 80 percent of vanilla is now produced in Madagascar it's rare to find Mexican vanilla at your local grocery store. I always stock up when I'm in Mexico, but you can also order it online. Gaya brand, made by my friend Norma Gaya who runs her family's vanilla plantation in Gutiérrez Zamora in the state of Veracruz, is the one I always recommend.

CINNAMON

In Mexico, when cooks use cinnamon, it's Ceylon cinnamon they reach for. Ceylon cinnamon is much milder and more delicate in flavor and aroma than the cassia cinnamon that is most often seen in the US. If you can't find Ceylon cinnamon in your grocery store, substitute with cassia and just use half the amount called for, or buy it online.

DRIED MEXICAN OREGANO

Despite its name, Mexican oregano is actually a member of the verbena family and not at all related to true oregano. Confusing, right? Its flavor is much brighter and more citrus-y than Mediterranean oregano so it lends itself well to Mexican dishes, which often feature fresh lemon or lime juice. Many larger grocery store chains have begun to stock Mexican oregano, and you can always find it at any Latin market or online. If you can't track it down, you can substitute regular dried oregano or marjoram.

DRIED BEANS

I always have dried pinto beans in my cupboard to make my Bacony Borracho Beans (page 241) and Refried Borracho Beans (page 242).

RO-TEL

I grew up with Ro-Tel, which is a brand of canned diced tomatoes mixed with green chiles, and always have cans of it in my pantry. It's such a Tex-Mex staple and adds lots of spicy flavor to beans and soups. If you can't find Ro-Tel, use any canned tomatoes with green chiles or chop up some fresh jalapeño or serrano and add to regular diced tomatoes.

TOMATO SAUCE

I often use canned tomato sauce when I don't have time to make my own sofrito for things like soups and Picadillo (page 96). Any grocery store-brand tomato sauce will work. If I want a little more spice, I'll sometimes swap in El Pato brand tomato sauce (made with hot chiles), which you can find in the Latin section of many grocery stores, at most Latin grocers, or online.

PICKLED JALAPEÑOS

I reach for these all the time to add spice and tang to things like tacos, tostadas, Hot Dogs el Galán (page 177), and Refried Bean and Jalapeño Tamales (page 137). I like Rio Luna brand because they're not toooo spicy but whatever your grocery store has will work.

CANNED CHIPOTLE PEPPERS IN ADOBO SAUCE

These are smoked jalapeños that are packed in a sweet and tangy sauce made of tomato, garlic, vinegar, and spices. The chiles add smoky spice to so many dishes in this book, including my Chipotle BBQ Sauce (page 165), Black Bean Stew with Pork (page 52), and Chicken Tinga (page 93), and the adobo sauce is the key ingredient in the Chipotle Crema (page 109) and the sauce for the Tuna Tostadas (page 99). These days, you can find canned chipotles in adobo in most grocery stores, but you can also always order them online.

CHICKEN AND VEGGIE BOUILLON CUBES

Almost every Mexican household has chicken bouillon cubes in the pantry. They lend salty, savory oomph to just about any soup or stew. I throw them into my Bacony Borracho Beans (page 241), Vegetable Soup with Squash Blossoms (page 69), Fideo Soup (page 61), or anything that could use a little extra flavor.

RICE

While there aren't any recipes for rice in this book, it's an essential pantry staple for me, so I had to include it. I always have long-grain white rice on hand so I can cook it plain or make it into Mexican rice (there's a good recipe in my first cookbook!). Serve it alongside Bacony Borracho Beans (page 241) with just about any meal.

SALT

I use kosher salt and flaky salt throughout this book, but because most recipes call for seasoning to taste, you can use whatever salt you prefer. For the few recipes that do call for a precise measurement of salt, use Diamond Crystal kosher salt to make sure the seasoning is correct. If you use Morton kosher, reduce the quantity by half.

DRIED CHILES

I use a lot of dried chiles at home, but for this book, I stuck to three widely available ones to keep things simple: guajillo, ancho, and árbol. You should be able to find these at many grocery stores, and any Latin market will certainly stock them. You can also order them online. When shopping for dried chiles, give them a little squeeze through the bag—if they feel brittle, they're likely old and won't have great flavor. Look for dried chiles that have a nice, deep color and are still a little soft. Guajillo taste bright, fruity, and spicy; ancho (which are dried poblano chiles) are smoky and fairly mild; and árbol are quite spicy (almost as hot as cayenne) with a slightly grassy and nutty flavor.

OLIVE OIL

I use good Spanish extra-virgin olive oil for pretty much everything—searing, sautéing, salad dressings, and finishing. And for frying, I use a good regular (not extra-virgin) one. Because olive oil has a slightly lower smoke point than some other vegetable oils, just make sure you keep the temp under 400°F (if you're not sure what this looks like, a thermometer is a helpful tool to have on hand when deep-frying).

MASA HARINA

You can use any store-bought dried masa to make the recipes in this book as long as it's nixtamalized (see page 136)—just look on the bag to make sure. Maseca is the most common brand, but I especially love the heirloom corn masa harina from Masienda.

Resources

DRIED BEANS
Rancho Gordo
ranchogordo.com

Primary Beans
primarybeans.com

DRIED CHILES AND SPICES
Don Juan Chiles
donjuanchiles.com

EXTRA-VIRGIN OLIVE OIL
Marqués de Valdueza
marquesdevaldueza.com/en/oil/

MASA HARINA
Masienda
masienda.com

Tamoa
tamoa.mx

Alma Semillera
almasemillera.com/collections
/dried-flowers

SPICES
Loisa
loisa.com

TORTILLA PRESS
Victoria Cookware
victoriacookware.com

Masienda
masienda.com

VANILLA EXTRACT
Gaya
gayamexico.com/en

**VANILLA EXTRACT AND
CONCHA CUTTER**
Lola's Cocina
lolascocina.com

PRODUCE

CILANTRO

I use cilantro to garnish just about everything (and always feel so bad for the people who think it tastes like soap!). Store like a bouquet of flowers in a jar of water in the fridge—it will add color and fragrance to your kitchen and delicious flavor to all your food.

LEMONS AND LIMES

I'm obsessed with citrus and always have lots of fresh lemons and limes on my counter for mixing margaritas, making guacamole, squeezing over tacos, or zesting into sauces.

FRESH CHILES

I always keep jalapeños and serranos in my fridge. They hold up so well and add fresh heat to everything from salsas to soups to tacos . . . not to mention my famous Flamin' Hot Margarita (page 215)!

TOOLS

TORTILLA PRESS

I use this for making corn tortillas plus pretty much everything in my masa chapter—gorditas, huaraches, tlacoyos, etc. They are affordable and last forever, but if you don't want to make the investment, you can always use your hands or a heavy pan to shape the masa.

ROLLING PIN

An essential tool for rolling out my flour tortillas! I prefer a traditional, nontapered wooden one.

CONCHA CUTTER

I usually cut decorations into my concha crust using a sharp knife, but these cutters, which can be easily found online, make beautiful, uniform shell shapes.

SLOW COOKER

I cannot live without my slow cooker. I use it for my Chicken Tinga (page 93), Slow Cooker Pork Ribs (page 164), and Bacony Borracho Beans (page 241), among other things.

MOLINILLO

These special wooden whisks are specifically designed for whipping up chocolate drinks, ensuring the maximum amount of froth. They are still used throughout the country and are a fun and beautiful addition to any home kitchen. If you can't find a molinillo, you can, of course, use a metal whisk to make my Champurrado (page 204), but I can't guarantee it will taste the same!

COMAL

A comal, which comes from the Nahuatl word *comalli*, is a smooth, flat-bottomed pan with shallow sides that was used in Mesoamerican kitchens. Traditionally made of Mexican clay, comals can now be found made of ceramic, cast iron, copper, and carbon steel. I love my cast-iron comal that I bought in Mexico City, but if you don't have one, any well-seasoned cast-iron pan, or even a large nonstick skillet, will work in any of the recipes that call for one.

DESAYUNO

10 Reasons to <u>Not</u> Skip Breakfast

I'll never understand the Western European approach to breakfast. For a place that celebrates and reveres food so much, breakfast often feels like an afterthought—something quick and sweet to eat with coffee—if it's thought of at all. It's the same in much of America, where many skip breakfast altogether or grab a quick bite on their way into work. If I eat a croissant or muffin first thing, I'm hungry in an hour.

In Mexico, however, breakfast is an event. The dishes are hot and filling and given the same care and attention as any other meal, maybe even more. There are fresh salsas, runny egg yolks, hot tortillas, crunchy totopos—spice, texture, and tons of flavor! In fact, many of the most popular breakfast foods, like Molletes (page 28) and Enfrijoladas (page 37), are also often served for lunch or dinner, too. But the thing I love even more than the food (which I really love) is the fact that in Mexico, breakfast is a meal you share, usually with family. I didn't grow up this way, but my Mexican husband did. And now my son, Santi, does, too, because no matter where in the world we are (or who might be staying with us!), my husband, Pepe, insists that everyone wake up to share breakfast—talking, eating, and laughing together. I can't think of a better way to start the day.

CHILAQUILES

Chilaquiles vary from region to region and house to house, but no matter how you make them—with salsa roja or verde; crunchy totopos or soaked and soft; with chicken; chorizo; fried eggs, or all of the above—they always hit the spot. I usually make them on the weekends and like mine crispy and smothered in salsa verde, topped with fried eggs, crema, queso fresco, and a little sliced onion to finish. When I have time, I make these with fresh Totopos (page 248), but good-quality store-bought tortilla chips work well in a pinch. Just be sure to look for thick ones, so they don't turn to mush in the sauce.

SERVES 2

2 tablespoons plus ¼ cup extra-virgin olive oil

1 cup Tomatillo Salsa (page 234) or your favorite store-bought green salsa

4 large eggs

Kosher salt and freshly ground black pepper

4 ounces fresh Totopos (page 248) or good-quality tortilla chips (about 5 cups)

¼ cup crumbled queso fresco

Mexican crema, for serving

Chopped fresh cilantro, for serving

Thinly sliced white onion rings, for serving

In a large skillet, heat 2 tablespoons of the olive oil over medium heat. Add the salsa and ¼ cup water and cook, stirring often, until the sauce is bubbling, about 2 minutes. Keep warm.

In a 12-inch nonstick skillet (preferably one with a lid), heat the remaining ¼ cup olive oil over high heat. When the oil is shimmery and hot but not smoking, carefully crack in the eggs (watch out—the oil might spit!) and quickly season with salt and pepper. Cook until the edges of the whites are crispy and start to brown, about 1 minute. Turn off the heat, carefully add 1 tablespoon water to the side of the pan, and cover with a lid (or baking sheet in a pinch). Let sit until the whites are set but the yolks are still runny, about 1 more minute. If your yolks are where you want them but your whites are still a little runny, spoon a little of the hot oil over the whites to help them finish cooking. Slide them onto a plate to stop the cooking.

Add the totopos to the pan with the salsa and quickly toss just to coat and warm them through (don't worry if all the chips don't get coated).

Divide the chilaquiles between two plates and add any salsa left in the pan. Top each with 2 fried eggs, the crumbled queso fresco, a drizzle of crema, some fresh cilantro, and a little sliced onion. Eat immediately.

POTATO AND EGG BREAKFAST TACOS

As a proud Texican, of course I had to include a breakfast taco recipe in my breakfast chapter! This mainstay of Northern Mexico and the American states that border it is the perfect on-the-go breakfast. In Monterrey—considered by many to be the epicenter of breakfast taco culture—you can choose from just about any fillings, from egg and chorizo to bean and cheese, potato and egg, barbacoa, the list goes on and on. One thing is for certain: Don't expect a corn tortilla! In the north, it's always flour. Everyone loves the potato and egg version, so this recipe is in heavy rotation in my house.

SERVES 4

½ cup good-quality olive oil (not extra-virgin)

2 medium Yukon Gold potatoes, peeled and cut into ¼- to ½-inch dice

½ medium white onion, diced

1 teaspoon garlic powder

1 teaspoon onion powder

Kosher salt and freshly ground black pepper

4 large eggs

8 small (4- to 5-inch) or 4 large (7- to 8-inch) flour tortillas, homemade (page 244) or store-bought

Optional garnishes: chopped fresh cilantro, chopped white onion, hot sauce, Tomatillo Salsa (page 234), Chipotle Salsa (page 230)

In a large (10- or 12-inch) nonstick skillet, heat the olive oil over medium heat. Add the potatoes, onion, garlic powder, and onion powder and season generously with salt and pepper. Cook gently, stirring often, until the onions are soft and the potatoes are tender, 15 to 20 minutes.

Crack the eggs into a bowl, season with salt and pepper, and whisk together. When the potatoes and onions are cooked, tilt the pan to the side and use a soup spoon to carefully remove any excess oil. Pour the eggs over the potato mixture and into the pan and cook, stirring often, until just set but still very soft, 1 to 2 minutes.

While the eggs cook, quickly heat the flour tortillas in a comal or skillet, flipping often, until soft and pliable.

Divide the filling among the warm tortillas and serve with your choice of garnishes.

MOLLETES

I grew up eating flour tortillas with refried beans for breakfast every morning. It just might be my number one comfort food. So anytime I see a breakfast dish with refried beans, I have to try it. Molletes, in their simplest and most classic form, are a split bolillo (a crusty white roll similar to a French roll) toasted in a pan with butter (the best way!) and topped with refried beans, quesillo cheese (which is also called Oaxaca cheese in the US and has the texture of mozzarella or string cheese and tastes similar to Monterey Jack cheese), and Pico de Gallo (page 231). It's so simple yet so filling and delicious. These make a perfect breakfast, lunch, or quick dinner, and can also be topped with cooked meats, fresh or roasted veggies, fried eggs, avocado, or anything else in your fridge!

SERVES 2 TO 4

2 bolillo rolls or French sandwich rolls

2 tablespoons unsalted butter, at room temperature

1 cup Bacony Borracho Beans (page 241) or canned refried black or pinto beans

1 cup freshly grated quesillo (Oaxaca cheese), Monterey Jack, or mozzarella cheese

½ to 1 cup Pico de Gallo (page 231), to taste

Preheat the oven to 400°F.

Cut the bolillos in half lengthwise and spread each half with ½ tablespoon butter. Heat a large skillet over medium-high heat. Add the bolillo halves, butter-side down (you will likely have to do this in batches), and cook until nicely toasted, 1 to 2 minutes.

Transfer the bread to a baking sheet, butter-side up. Dividing evenly, spread the refried beans over each half. Top with grated cheese and bake until the beans are hot and the cheese is melted, about 5 minutes.

Top with pico and serve immediately.

CONCHAS

Conchas are my happy place. I love the combination of the rich, lightly sweetened dough and crunchy sugary topping, carefully decorated to look like a giant edible scallop shell. Growing up, I got these sweet and yeasty breakfast buns from the local panadería—5 for $1, slightly stale, and probably packed with preservatives—so the first time I ate a made-from-scratch concha straight out of the oven, I was in heaven. I developed this recipe so I could enjoy the warm hug only a fresh concha can give even when I'm not in Mexico. And now you can, too!

The technique is very simple, but they do take about 4 hours to make from start to finish, so plan ahead. These are life-changing eaten warm but will keep well for up to 4 days in an airtight container on the counter. You can eat them at room temp, but they're even better quickly reheated in a warm oven or toaster oven for a few minutes.

MAKES 12 CONCHAS

CONCHA DOUGH

1 stick (4 ounces) unsalted butter

3¾ cups all-purpose flour, plus more for shaping

⅓ cup sugar

2½ teaspoons instant yeast

2 teaspoons kosher salt

½ cup whole milk, at room temperature

3 large eggs, at room temperature

2 teaspoons vanilla extract (preferably Mexican)

1 teaspoon extra-virgin olive oil

TOPPING

1 stick (4 ounces) unsalted butter, at room temperature

1 cup all-purpose flour

⅓ cup sugar

Pinch of kosher salt

Make the concha dough: In small saucepan, melt the butter over low heat, being careful not to brown it. Once completely melted, set aside to cool while you prepare the other ingredients.

In the bowl of a stand mixer, combine the flour, sugar, yeast, and salt and whisk together by hand. Attach the dough hook.

In a separate bowl, whisk together the milk, eggs, and vanilla. Pour into the flour mixture, add the melted and cooled butter, and mix on medium speed until the dough is smooth and pulls away from the sides of the bowl, about 10 minutes.

Lightly oil a large bowl with the olive oil, transfer the dough to the bowl, cover with a clean kitchen towel, and let rest until the dough doubles in size. The time will vary depending on how hot or cool your kitchen is, but it should take 2 to 2½ hours.

While the dough rests, make the topping: In a medium bowl, combine the butter, flour, sugar, and salt and use your fingers or a wooden spoon to mix until smooth, 2 to 3 minutes. Roll the mixture into a rough log, wrap in plastic wrap, and place in the fridge to chill for at least 30 minutes.

(continued on next page)

When the dough has doubled in size, arrange racks in the upper and lower thirds of the oven and preheat to 350°F. Line two baking sheets with parchment paper.

Remove the topping from the fridge to warm up.

Use your fist to punch down the dough, pressing into the center to release the air. Remove the dough from the bowl and place on a lightly floured work surface. Divide the dough into 12 equal portions. Lightly flour a clean work surface and, working one at a time, gently and loosely cup your hand over the piece of dough. Leaving your fingertips on the work surface, move your hand around in small circles, letting the base of the dough ball stick to the work surface and the shape of your hand push and pull the dough into a smooth ball. As you work, divide the dough balls between the prepared baking sheets and cover with clean kitchen towels to keep them from drying out.

Set a timer for 1 hour and begin work on the topping. Cut the log into 12 equal slices. Place them, one at a time, between your palms and press, flattening roughly into rounds 4 inches across and ¼ inch thick. This part takes a little practice! If your hands are hot, the topping might tear a bit, but don't be discouraged—you can always roll each piece back into a little ball and start again. I find the palm technique works best, but some prefer to roll these out between lightly oiled pieces of parchment paper or plastic wrap. Play around and see what works best for you.

As you press or roll out your toppings, drape each over a resting dough ball, carefully pressing the topping into the sides a bit to make sure it sticks. When all of the conchas have been topped, use a sharp knife or concha cutter to carve a shell design into the sugary crust, being careful just to score the topping and not to cut into the dough beneath. Return the kitchen towels and let them finish their 1-hour rest.

Remove the towels, transfer the baking sheets to the oven, and bake until they smell incredible and are lightly golden brown, 18 to 20 minutes, switching racks and rotating the sheets front to back halfway through.

Eat right away (as if I needed to tell you that!).

HUEVOS RANCHEROS

 I'm a rancher's daughter, so I have a soft spot for this dish. And because I order it so often, I fancy myself a bit of a connoisseur. After eating lots, and I mean lots, of plates of huevos rancheros over the years, I've developed my own go-to recipe: gently fried tortilla, refried borracho beans, fried eggs, and a perfectly balanced ranchero sauce poured over the top.

SERVES 2 TO 4

¼ cup extra-virgin olive oil

4 corn tortillas, homemade (page 247) or store-bought

1 cup Refried Borracho Beans (page 242) or canned refried pinto beans, warmed

4 large eggs

Kosher salt and freshly ground black pepper

1 cup Ranchero Sauce (recipe follows), warmed

Optional garnishes: sliced avocado, queso fresco, chopped fresh cilantro

Line a plate with paper towels and have near the stove. In a 12-inch nonstick deep skillet (preferably one with a lid), heat the olive oil over medium-high heat. Add the corn tortillas one at a time and cook, carefully flipping with tongs, for 10 seconds per side, until soft and just starting to blister (or you can leave a little longer if you like them crispier). Transfer to the paper towels to soak up any excess oil.

Divide the tortillas among serving plates and top each one with ¼ cup of refried beans.

Increase the heat under the skillet to high and when the oil is shimmery and hot but not smoking, carefully crack in the eggs (watch out—the oil might spit!) and season with salt and pepper. Cook until the edges of the whites are crispy and starting to brown, about 1 minute. Turn off the heat, carefully add 1 tablespoon of water to the side of the skillet, and cover with a lid (or baking sheet in a pinch). Let the eggs steam until the whites are set but the yolks are still runny, about 1 more minute. Remove the cover—if your yolks are where you want them, but your whites are still a little runny, spoon a little of the hot oil from the pan over the whites to help them finish cooking.

Slide an egg on top of each tortilla and spoon over the ranchero sauce. If desired, serve with avocado, queso fresco, and/or cilantro.

(continued on next page)

Ranchero Sauce

MAKES ABOUT 2½ CUPS

2 tablespoons extra-virgin
olive oil
1 medium white onion, diced
Kosher salt and freshly ground
black pepper
3 large garlic cloves, minced
1 medium jalapeño, seeded and
minced
2 teaspoons ancho chile
powder
1 teaspoon dried Mexican
oregano
1 teaspoon ground cumin
1 (14.5-ounce) can diced
tomatoes, undrained
1 canned chipotle pepper in
adobo sauce
¼ cup roughly chopped fresh
cilantro
1¼ cups chicken stock or water

In a large sauté pan or
medium Dutch oven, heat
the oil over medium-high
heat. Add the onion, season
with salt and pepper, and
cook, stirring often, until
translucent and starting to
brown, 5 to 7 minutes. Add
the garlic, jalapeño, chile
powder, oregano, and cumin
and cook until fragrant,
about 1 minute.

Stir in the diced tomatoes
with their juices, chipotle
pepper, cilantro, and chicken
stock. Season to taste with
more salt and pepper.
Bring the mixture to a boil,
then reduce to a simmer
and cook, uncovered, for
20 minutes to thicken the
sauce and meld the flavors.

Use an immersion blender
(or transfer to a stand
blender) to blend the sauce
until smooth.

Taste for seasoning and
either use immediately or
cool and store in the fridge
for up to 1 week or in the
freezer for up to 3 months.

ENFRIJOLADAS

There's an expression in Mexico—*bañado*, to be "bathed in." I was used to "bathing" my tortillas in red sauce for enchiladas, but until Pepe introduced me to this dish, I'd never heard of anything being bathed in a sauce made of beans! Que rico! This dish is similar to enchiladas (fried tortillas are dipped in sauce and rolled), but here, the sauce is the star. After being rolled up with whatever fillings you like (some classics are crumbled queso fresco or shredded chicken), the dish is then drowned in more sauce before serving. They are often made with black beans, but because I always have some cooked Bacony Borracho Beans (page 241) in my fridge, that's what I usually use. If you're using canned beans, add a teaspoon each of garlic powder and onion powder to the blender to give them a little more flavor.

SERVES 2 TO 4

1½ cups Bacony Borracho Beans (page 241) or 1 (15-ounce) can black beans, drained and rinsed

1 cup bean cooking liquid, chicken stock, or water

2 canned chipotle peppers plus 1 tablespoon adobo sauce from the can

Kosher salt and freshly ground black pepper

2 tablespoons plus ¼ cup extra-virgin olive oil

8 corn tortillas, homemade (page 247) or store-bought

4 ounces crumbled queso fresco, plus more for garnish

Chopped fresh cilantro, for garnish

In a high-powered blender, combine the cooked beans, bean liquid, chipotle peppers, and adobo sauce. Blend until very smooth, 2 to 3 minutes. Season to taste with salt and pepper.

In a medium sauté pan, heat the 2 tablespoons of the olive oil over medium heat. Pour in the bean sauce and cook, stirring often, until the sauce is bubbling and has thickened slightly, about 5 minutes. Turn off the heat and cover to keep warm.

Line a large plate with paper towels and set near the stove. In a small saucepan or skillet just wide enough to hold 1 tortilla, heat the remaining ¼ cup olive oil over medium-high heat. Working with 1 tortilla at a time, add to the pan and cook, carefully flipping with tongs, until soft and just starting to blister, about 10 seconds per side. Remove to the paper towels to soak up any excess oil.

When ready to serve, dip each tortilla in the bean sauce, then transfer to a large plate or platter. Fill with 2 tablespoons of the queso fresco and either roll up like a little taquito or fold the tortilla in half. Transfer to a serving plate or platter. Continue dipping, filling, and rolling until you've used up all the tortillas.

Spoon the remaining bean sauce over the top and garnish with more queso fresco and some chopped cilantro.

MEXICAN FRENCH TOAST
with Piloncillo Syrup and Pecans

In Spanish we have an expression *vale la pena*, which roughly translates to "to be worth it." I don't have much of a sweet tooth, so if I'm eating something sweet for breakfast it must vale la pena! This French toast certainly qualifies.

I've been making this for years, usually for weekend breakfasts when family or friends are in town. This recipe isn't traditionally Mexican (obviously—it has *French* in the title!), but I put my Mexican twist on it with piloncillo sugar and Mexican vanilla. If you can't find piloncillo sugar, feel free to substitute brown sugar, but the Mexican vanilla is nonnegotiable!

SERVES 4 TO 6

4 large eggs

4 tablespoons grated piloncillo or lightly packed light brown sugar

1 tablespoon Mexican vanilla extract

4 tablespoons unsalted butter, plus more as needed

1 (14-ounce) loaf brioche, cut into 6 (roughly 1½-inch) slices

3 ripe bananas, peeled and cut into ½-inch slices

½ cup maple syrup

½ cup chopped pecans, toasted first if you like

Preheat the oven to 200°F.

Crack the eggs into a shallow medium bowl. Add 2 tablespoons of the piloncillo and the vanilla and whisk until mostly smooth.

Heat a large sauté pan over medium heat and add 1 tablespoon of the butter. Dip a piece of brioche in the egg mixture and soak for about 5 seconds per side. Lift the brioche to let any excess drip off, then transfer to the pan and cook until beautifully golden brown, 1 to 2 minutes per side. Transfer to an ovenproof serving platter and set in the oven to keep warm. Continue soaking and browning, adding more butter to the pan as needed, until all the brioche is cooked.

Wipe out the pan with a paper towel and add 2 more tablespoons butter. When it's melted and starts to foam, add the remaining 2 tablespoons piloncillo and the sliced bananas. Cook, stirring gently (you don't want to break up the banana slices) and often, until the sugar has melted and the bananas are soft, 2 to 3 minutes.

Add the maple syrup and bring up to a simmer. Let the syrup mixture bubble gently for 1 to 2 minutes to thicken slightly. Turn off the heat and stir in the chopped pecans.

Carefully remove the serving platter from the oven, pour the topping over everything, and serve immediately.

Toasting Nuts and Seeds

To be honest, this is an extra step that I often skip myself. But if you do have a few minutes, toasting nuts and seeds gives them so much more flavor!

To do it, spread them out in an even layer on a baking sheet and bake in a 325°F oven for anywhere from 5 minutes (for something like pepitas or slivered almonds) to 10 minutes (for something larger like hazelnuts or whole almonds), giving them a stir about halfway through so they cook evenly and carefully watching them the entire time. When they start to smell delicious, look lightly golden, and are a little bit shiny, remove them and let them cool on the baking sheet.

You can toast nuts and seeds in advance and keep them in an airtight container in a cool, dark place (like your cupboard) for a few days.

Vanilla, the Edible Orchid

Although 80 percent of the world's vanilla is now harvested in Madagascar, the plant is endemic to Papantla, a lush and mountainous city in the state of Veracruz, on Mexico's Gulf coast. The Totonacs, the indigenous peoples of this region, were the first to cultivate it back in the twelfth century, and this regal spice has been venerated in Mexican culture ever since. According to Totonac legend, the vanilla orchid was born out of the tragic and forbidden love between a demigod princess and a mortal. Despite her father's orders, the princess and her lover ran away together, only to be captured and killed. Their blood dripped into the soil below and from it, the *Vanilla planifolia*—a beautiful plant with yellow flowers, strong vines, and a sweet perfume—grew.

For hundreds of years, Mexico had a monopoly on vanilla production, not only because the plant was native but because of a local bee whose sole job was to pollinate the flower, thus producing the precious vanilla bean. When the Spanish explorers arrived, they brought the orchid back to Europe and it eventually made its way around the world, including to Madagascar, Réunion, Tahiti, and Mauritius, where the soil and climate conditions were perfect for growing. The plants flourished, but without the Mexican bee, they wouldn't produce any vanilla pods, until a twelve-year-old boy named Edmond Albius developed a way to pollinate the flower by hand—a technique still referred to as "le geste d'Edmond"—and production began to take off in this part of the world. Around the same time, due to logging and the discovery of oil in the region, the extinction of the pollinating bee, and the Mexican Revolution, vanilla production in Mexico slowed considerably and many orchid fields were abandoned. Today, Mexico produces less than 1 percent of vanilla on the global market.

But insiders know that Mexican vanilla is unparalleled in flavor and quality, and many producers—like my friend Norma Gaya, who runs her family's 150-year-old vanilla plantation Gaya Vai-Mex in the mountains of Veracruz—are working hard to regain the country's reputation as a world leader.

CLARAS *a la Mexicana*

This is my husband's favorite way to eat eggs, which is great for me, because they're so easy to make! Essentially a quick scramble made with white onion, tomato, and fresh chile, the eggs offer a similarly bold bite as you'd find in a salsa-laden dish like Huevos Divorciados (page 42) or Chilaquiles (page 24), just not as heavy. And because Pepe's cholesterol is slightly high, I use egg whites to make mine even lighter. A bonus: I find that ditching the yolks allows the flavors of the chile, tomato, and onion to really shine through. Serve this bright and bold-tasting egg dish alone or scoop it onto a piece of toasted sourdough, called masa madre in Spanish.

SERVES 2

2 tablespoons extra-virgin olive oil

½ small white onion, minced (about 1 cup)

1 medium Roma tomato, finely chopped (about 1 cup)

Kosher salt and freshly ground black pepper

½ medium serrano chile, minced (seeded if you want less heat)

6 large egg whites

In a medium nonstick skillet, heat the oil over medium-high heat. Add the onion and tomato, season with salt and black pepper, and cook, stirring often, until the juice from the tomato has evaporated and the onion has started to soften, 3 to 5 minutes. Add the serrano and cook until just beginning to soften, about another 30 seconds.

In a medium bowl, season the egg whites with salt and pepper and give them a good whisk to combine. Reduce the heat to medium, add the egg whites to the pan, and cook gently, stirring constantly with a spatula or wooden spoon, until set, 1 to 2 minutes. Serve.

HUEVOS DIVORCIADOS

Huevos divorciados means, you guessed it, "divorced eggs." Even before I tried this dish, I loved it for its cute and clever name. Inspired by huevos rancheros, the twist here is that one fried egg is drowned in red salsa and one in green. I can never choose between red or green salsa on my eggs—I can't! I can't! Don't make me do it!!—and now I never have to.

SERVES 2

¼ cup extra-virgin olive oil

4 corn tortillas, homemade (page 247) or store-bought

4 large eggs

Kosher salt and freshly ground black pepper

½ cup Chipotle Salsa (page 230) or your favorite store-bought red salsa, warmed

½ cup Tomatillo Salsa (page 234) or your favorite store-bought green salsa, warmed

Line a plate with paper towels and set near the stove. In a 12-inch nonstick deep skillet (preferably one with a lid), heat the olive oil over medium-high heat. Add the corn tortillas one at a time and cook, carefully flipping with tongs, until soft and just starting to blister, about 10 seconds per side. Remove to the paper towels to soak up any excess oil.

Divide the tortillas between two plates.

Turn the heat up to high under the skillet and when the oil is shimmery and hot but not smoking, carefully crack in the eggs (watch out—the oil might spit!) and season with salt and pepper. Cook until the edges of the whites are crispy and starting to brown, about 1 minute. Turn off the heat, carefully add 1 tablespoon of water to the side of the pan, and cover with a lid (or baking sheet in a pinch). Let sit until the whites are set but the yolks are still runny, about 1 more minute. If your yolks are where you want them, but your whites are still a little runny, spoon a little of the hot oil from the pan over the whites to help them finish cooking. Remove to a plate to stop the cooking.

Top each tortilla with a fried egg. Spoon half of the red salsa over one egg on each plate and half of the green salsa on the other.

HUEVOS CON JOCOQUE, *My Style*

Starting in the late nineteenth century and into the early twentieth century, many Lebanese immigrants, initially driven out of their homeland by the unstable Ottoman regime, began coming to Mexico. They entered through the ports along the gulf and settled mostly nearby along the Yucatán Peninsula, in Veracruz, Puebla, and Mexico City, and up into the northern part of the country, bringing much of their food and culture with them.

You'll find Lebanese roots throughout Mexican cuisine if you know where to look and one of my favorite examples is huevos con jocoque, also sometimes called huevos Árabes, or huevos Libaneses. In the original dish, eggs are sprinkled with za'atar, fried in a small clay bowl, or cazuela, and then served alongside jocoque (a fermented dairy product) with raw white onion, fresh serrano chile, and pita bread on the side.

Because I can almost never find jocoque, I use Greek yogurt instead. I also swap in garlic and lemon for the bite of white onion and drizzle my salsa macha over it all for texture and heat. It's sooooo good. Serve this with pita or a slice of sourdough on the side for scooping.

SERVES 2

1 cup whole-milk Greek yogurt

1 medium garlic clove, grated or minced

Grated zest and juice of ½ medium lemon

Kosher salt and freshly ground black pepper

¼ cup extra-virgin olive oil

4 large eggs

½ teaspoon za'atar

Salsa Macha (page 237), for serving

Chopped fresh cilantro, for garnish

In a medium bowl, combine the yogurt, garlic, lemon zest, lemon juice, and salt and pepper to taste. Divide between two shallow bowls or plates, spreading it out a bit with a spoon to make a nice bed for the eggs.

In a 12-inch nonstick skillet (preferably one with a lid), heat the olive oil over high heat. When the oil is shimmery and hot but not smoking, carefully crack in the eggs (watch out— the oil might spit!) and quickly season with the za'atar and salt and pepper. Cook until the edges of the whites are crispy and starting to brown, about 1 minute. Turn off the heat, carefully add a tablespoon of water to the side of the pan, and cover with a lid (or baking sheet in a pinch). Let steam until the whites are set but the yolks are still runny, about 1 more minute. If your yolks are where you want them, but your whites are still a little runny, spoon a little of the hot oil from the pan over the whites to help them finish cooking.

Transfer the eggs to the serving dishes and top with salsa macha and cilantro.

SOPAS
THAT SATISFY

Growing up in the south Texas heat, we didn't eat a lot of soup. When we did, it was occasionally Campbell's chicken noodle, and more often Wolf Brand Chili, served with saltine crackers or spooned over Fritos to make the classic Tex-Mex delicacy Frito pie. I honestly didn't even know you could make soup from scratch—I thought it only came out of a can! Imagine my surprise when I started cooking, traveling, and discovering the vast world of homemade soups. The first time I made Lentil Soup with Fideo and Roasted Eggplant (page 62) or my Sopa de Lima (page 66), I swear you would have thought that I'd found gold in the West.

My love affair has only deepened over the years, and now I'm proud to say that I am, and will always be, a year-round soup kind of girl. I've also become a soup-as-a-meal kind of girl. I don't believe in reserving soups for cold weather, or only eating them to stave off colds and flus. A quality soup—hearty and brothy and bursting with good-for-you ingredients—is one of the most satisfying meals I can think of.

In this chapter, you'll find a mix of slow-simmered stews, pozole with all the fixings, quick and healthy veggie soups, and everything in between, usually served with a colorful array of condiments, like fresh lime, chopped white onion, spicy salsas, diced avocado, and crispy tortilla strips, to make each bowl your own.

ALBÓNDIGAS

I love a meatball soup from any country and this albóndigas, which actually originated in Spain but is popular throughout Mexico, just might be my favorite. The meatballs, seasoned with cumin and fresh cilantro and bound with rice rather than bread crumbs, simmer in a broth tinged red from tomatoes (or Ro-Tel, if you like it spicy) along with potato, zucchini, and any other vegetables you happen to have in the fridge. This simple soup is deceptively delicious, and something the whole family can enjoy. It's also an easy one to prep in advance—make and shape the meatballs and chop the veggies up to a day or two ahead, then throw everything together when you get home.

SERVES 6 TO 8

MEATBALLS
2 tablespoons extra-virgin olive oil

½ medium yellow onion, diced

1 pound ground beef (I like 80/20)

½ cup cooked white rice, cooled

1 tablespoon garlic powder

1 teaspoon ground cumin

1 teaspoon kosher salt

½ teaspoon freshly ground black pepper

1 large egg, lightly beaten

¼ cup finely chopped fresh cilantro

Make the meatballs: In a medium sauté pan, heat the olive oil over medium-high heat. Add the onion and cook, stirring often, until translucent and starting to brown, 5 to 7 minutes. Transfer to a bowl to cool.

While the onion cools, in a separate medium bowl, combine the ground beef, cooked rice, garlic powder, cumin, salt, pepper, egg, and cilantro.

Stir the cooled onion into the beef mixture and mix to combine. Roll into 1-inch balls, place on a large plate or small baking sheet, and cover with plastic wrap or a clean kitchen towel and set aside while you make the soup (or transfer to the fridge for later).

Make the soup: In a soup pot or large Dutch oven, heat the olive oil over medium-high heat. Add the onion, season with salt and pepper, and cook, stirring often, until translucent and starting to brown, 5 to 7 minutes.

Add the celery and carrots and cook until starting to soften, about 5 minutes. Stir in the garlic, cumin, and oregano and cook until fragrant, about 1 minute. Add the diced tomatoes (or Ro-Tel) and their juices and cook, stirring often, until most of the juices have evaporated, 3 to 5 minutes.

(continued on next page)

3 tablespoons extra-virgin olive oil

½ medium yellow onion, diced

Kosher salt and freshly ground black pepper

2 medium celery stalks, diced

2 medium carrots, diced

5 medium garlic cloves, minced

1 tablespoon ground cumin

1 teaspoon dried Mexican oregano

1 (14.5-ounce) can diced tomatoes or 2 (10-ounce) cans Ro-Tel, undrained

2 medium Yukon Gold potatoes, peeled and cut into 1-inch pieces

8 cups chicken or beef broth, or 4 cups My Go-To Bone Broth (opposite) diluted with 4 cups water

1 medium zucchini, cut into ¾-inch pieces

½ cup frozen green peas

Chopped fresh cilantro

Lemon or lime wedges, for squeezing

Add the potatoes, broth, and a few generous pinches of salt. Bring the soup up to a simmer and cook until the potatoes are starting to soften, about 10 minutes.

Taste for seasoning then carefully drop in the meatballs, moving them around as needed to make sure they're submerged in the broth. Return to a simmer and gently cook until the potatoes are very tender and most of the meatballs have floated up to the top, about 10 minutes.

Add the zucchini and frozen peas, bring back up to a simmer, and cook until the zucchini is just tender and the meatballs are cooked through, about 5 minutes. Taste for seasoning.

Serve topped with fresh cilantro, with lemon or lime wedges for squeezing.

MY GO-TO BONE BROTH

I started making my own bone broth because I was tired of the flavorless boxed stock I was getting from the grocery store. At first, I tried doctoring the store-bought stuff with more salt and spices, but no matter how much I tried, it always just tasted like, well, nothing special. Bone broth is another story. It tastes delicious and complex (definitely sabroso!), adds great backbone to any soup, and is filling and flavorful enough to drink on its own.

We eat a lot of rotisserie chicken in my house, so instead of tossing the bones (which always felt wasteful anyway), I started saving the carcasses and turning them into a broth at the end of the week. Wow, what a difference! This stuff is liquid gold. And because it simmers for hours over low heat, the gelatin and protein in the bones gets pulled out, leaving you with a delicious and super nutrient-dense broth.

I always have some of this in the freezer to add to soups and stews, and it's so good sipped plain, too. Feel free to change up the aromatics depending on what you like and what you have in the fridge; sometimes I'll add fresh thyme, sometimes fresh ginger and ground turmeric (or fresh if I can find it).

Because the bones cook down for hours, be sure to start with bones from the best-quality chickens you can. And if you don't go through rotisserie chickens at quite the same rate as my family, you can always freeze the carcasses until you have enough for a batch.

MAKES ABOUT 3 QUARTS

Carcasses of 2 roast chickens or rotisserie chickens

3 scallions, trimmed but whole

2 medium carrots

2 medium celery stalks

½ large yellow or white onion

2 dried bay leaves

1 tablespoon kosher salt, plus more as needed

1 teaspoon black peppercorns

In a stockpot or large Dutch oven, combine the carcasses, scallions, carrots, celery, onion, bay leaves, salt, and peppercorns. Cover with water (about 5 quarts) and bring to a boil. Use a slotted spoon or skimmer to remove any scum or other impurities that come up to the surface.

Reduce the heat to maintain a very low simmer and cook, topping with water as needed to make sure everything is submerged, until the broth is deeply golden and has reduced by about one-third, about 8 hours.

Carefully strain into a large, heatproof bowl and taste for seasoning, adding more salt if needed. Cool to room temperature, then transfer to glass jars and store in the fridge for up to 4 days or in the freezer (just be sure not to overfill the jars because the broth will expand a bit!) for up to 3 months.

BLACK BEAN STEW *with Pork*

On one of my trips to the Yucatán Peninsula, I was lucky enough to get a tour of the ancient Mayan city of Uxmal from local archaeologist Don Pepe. After admiring the remarkable craftsmanship and intricate detail of the ceremonial ruins, we went back to his "base camp" for lunch: a melt-in-your-mouth pork and black bean stew. Since much of the Yucatán is on the water (Cancún, on the Mexican Riviera . . .), I had assumed many Yucatecan dishes would center on fish, but because it spoiled so quickly and easily in the days before refrigeration, fish never became a staple of the local diet. So here, pork reigns supreme.

To make this dish, Don Pepe and his wife, Maria, first smoke the pork, then add dried black beans, a fresh herb called epazote (which is said to help alleviate gas), and a few good pinches of salt and cover it all with water. Next, they bury the pot in a píib—an underground pit heated with stones and wood traditionally used in this region (where the "pibil" in the famous Yucatecan pork dish cochinita pibil comes from!)—and cook it for 12 hours, until the meat is falling apart and the broth has taken on a wonderfully smoky flavor.

The moment I tasted it, I started thinking about how to re-create it at home (ideally without digging a giant hole in my backyard!). And voilà, I think I landed on something that evokes the original. The smokiness from the bacon mimics the smoked pork, the cilantro stands in for the epazote (but if you can find epazote in a Mexican market or grocery store, please use it), the chipotle pepper adds another layer of smoky flavor, and the pork shoulder is so tender it just falls apart. Like my hosts, I usually serve this with corn tortillas and lots of condiments on the side, letting everyone make their own bean and pork tacos while also spooning up the delicious broth.

1 pound boneless pork shoulder, trimmed of any excess fat and cut into 2-inch pieces

Kosher salt

2 slices bacon, diced

1 small white onion, diced

4 large garlic cloves, minced

1 teaspoon ground cumin

1½ cups dried black beans, rinsed and picked over

2 canned chipotle peppers plus 1 tablespoon adobo sauce from the can

1 handful cilantro sprigs (about ¼ bunch)

Freshly ground black pepper

Corn tortillas, homemade (page 247) or store-bought, warmed, for serving

Optional garnishes: diced radish, sliced avocado, chopped white onion, chopped fresh cilantro, lime wedges, spicy salsa

Pat the pork dry with a paper towel and add to a bowl. Season the pork with about 1 teaspoon kosher salt, tossing it to season all sides.

Heat a medium soup pot or Dutch oven over medium-high heat. Add the bacon and cook, stirring often, until crispy and browned, about 5 minutes.

Transfer the bacon to a large plate and add the pork shoulder pieces to the pot, cooking until all sides are nicely browned, about 10 minutes. Use a slotted spoon to transfer the pork to the same plate as the bacon. Add the onion to the fat in the pot and cook, stirring often, until translucent and starting to brown, about 5 minutes. Add the garlic and cumin and cook until fragrant, about 1 minute.

Stir in the black beans, chipotles, adobo sauce, cilantro sprigs, and 6 cups water. Return the bacon and pork shoulder to the pot along with any accumulated juices and season with 2 teaspoons kosher salt. Bring the mixture to a boil. Reduce to a simmer, partially cover, and cook until the beans are tender and the pork is falling apart, about 2½ hours.

Use tongs to remove the cilantro sprigs. Season to taste with salt and black pepper. Serve in bowls with corn tortillas and other garnishes on the side.

Beans of the New World

When it comes to beans, there are two main categories: Old World and New World. Old World beans, which are mostly native to the Mediterranean and Asia, include chickpeas, lentils (which are technically a legume), fava beans, soybeans, and adzuki beans. The New World beans, which include the common bean, runner bean, and lima bean, are endemic to the Americas and have played a major role in the local diet for over ten thousand years. Before the Spanish conquest in 1519, beans, which are easy to grow, cheap to buy, and full of protein, were one of the main food groups for many civilizations in Mesoamerica.

They were also, and continue to be, an essential part of the milpa, an ancient farming system used in Mexico and throughout Mesoamerica for thousands of years. The term *milpa* comes from the Nahuatl word *milpan*, which means "cultivated field," and usually refers to the practice of growing corn, squash, and beans (often called the "three sisters" in reference to these three indigenous crops) together. The corn provides strong stems to support climbing beans, the beans provide nitrogen to the soil, and the squash leaves smother the weeds and provide shade to keep the soil moist—they share the same resources and grow stronger together.

There were originally five native seeds for beans in Mexico and now, thanks to cultivation and hybridization, there are over two hundred varieties with different colors, textures, and flavor profiles. I always stock my pantry with dried pinto beans (which, along with black, kidney, and cannellini, are members of the common bean family), but I also love more specialty, heirloom varieties of *Phaseolus vulgaris* (the Latin name for common beans) like Rio Zape and Vaquero. These can be sourced from companies like Rancho Gordo and Primary Beans (see Resources, page 19), who work with smaller farmers in both the US and Mexico. Dried beans from these companies are consistently fresher and more flavorful than the ones you can get at the grocery store, and cook up so tender. Plus, they make hard-to-find indigenous varietals—like Ayocote beans, which were one of the first runner beans cultivated in the Americas—available with a quick click.

VEGGIE CHILI

As any true Texan knows, you gotta have a good chili recipe, and this is mine. It's my go-to Super Bowl dish and soccer day meal. You can put it on hot dogs, you can put it on a burger, you can eat it in a bowl. While Mexican chili, or chili con carne, is made with chunks of beef and/or pork slowly simmered in a dried chile sauce, my recipe is a little more Tex-Mex. Inspired by the canned chili I grew up eating, this vegan version is loaded with beans, fire-roasted tomatoes, and lots of spices. I love the combo of kidney, cannellini, and pinto beans, but any mix of canned beans works well here.

SERVES 6 TO 8

3 tablespoons extra-virgin olive oil

1 medium green bell pepper, diced

1 medium yellow bell pepper, diced

1 medium red bell pepper, diced

1 large yellow onion, diced

Kosher salt and freshly ground black pepper

4 large garlic cloves, minced

2 teaspoons ancho chile powder

2 teaspoons ground cumin

1 teaspoon onion powder

1 teaspoon garlic powder

½ teaspoon red pepper flakes

¼ teaspoon cayenne pepper

2 (14.5-ounce) cans diced fire-roasted tomatoes, undrained

1 (15-ounce) can kidney beans, drained and rinsed

1 (15-ounce) can cannellini beans, drained and rinsed

1 (15-ounce) can pinto beans, drained and rinsed

In a medium soup pot or Dutch oven, heat the oil over medium-high heat. Add the bell peppers and sauté, stirring often, until tender and starting to brown, about 5 minutes. Stir in the onion, season generously with salt and black pepper, and cook until translucent and starting to brown, about 5 minutes.

Add the garlic, ancho powder, cumin, onion powder, garlic powder, pepper flakes, and cayenne and cook until fragrant, about 1 minute. Stir in the canned tomatoes and their juices and cook for 5 minutes, stirring often to make sure nothing is sticking or burning in the bottom of the pot.

Add the beans and 4 cups water, season generously with salt and black pepper, and bring to a boil. Reduce the heat to a simmer and cook, uncovered, for 30 minutes to thicken the chili and meld the flavors.

Taste for seasoning and serve with your favorite garnishes (such as shredded cheddar cheese, diced avocado, diced onion, hot sauce, or tortilla chips) on the side.

CORN AND GREEN CHILE SOUP
with Salsa Macha

Because corn is so essential to Mexican cuisine and culture (see page 141), I felt it was important to include a corn soup in this book. I love slightly spicy green chiles and sweet corn on sopes or in tamales, so I decided to use them here—and the result is amazing. I could drink it straight from the pot. It's also quick to pull together and happens to be vegan if you skip the crema. Make this in the summertime when fresh corn is sweet, and don't forget the salsa macha!

SERVES 4 TO 6

4 ears sweet corn, shucked

2 tablespoons extra-virgin olive oil

1 medium white onion, diced

Kosher salt and freshly ground black pepper

4 large garlic cloves, roughly chopped

¼ cup chopped fresh cilantro stems, plus chopped leaves for serving

1 (7-ounce) can chopped green chiles, undrained

Mexican crema, for serving

Salsa Macha (page 237), for serving

One at a time, hold each ear of corn down flat on a cutting board and carefully slice off one side of the kernels. Turn the cob so the flat side is now resting on the cutting board and continue slicing and flipping until you've cut off all the kernels. Transfer the kernels to a bowl; reserve the cobs.

In a heavy-bottomed medium soup pot or Dutch oven, heat the oil over medium heat. Add the onion, season with salt and pepper, and cook, stirring occasionally, until translucent and starting to brown, 5 to 7 minutes. Stir in the garlic and cilantro stems and cook for another minute.

Add the green chiles and the juices and cook, stirring often, until most of their liquid has evaporated, another 5 minutes. Add 6 cups water and the reserved corn cobs, season generously with salt and pepper, and bring to a boil. Reduce the heat to a simmer and cook until the cobs have released some of their flavor, 10 to 15 minutes. Add the corn kernels, bring to a boil, then reduce to a simmer, cooking until the kernels are tender, another 15 minutes.

Discard the cobs. Carefully transfer some soup to a high-powered blender and blend until very smooth, about 3 minutes. Pour into a clean pot or bowl and repeat with the remaining soup. (Blend in batches to avoid the hot soup exploding from the blender!) Taste for seasoning and serve with a drizzle of crema, salsa macha, and chopped cilantro.

FIDEO SOUP

Ask any Mexican about sopa de fideo and chances are they'll give you some variation of this recipe. A staple in Mexican and Mexican American households, this simple yet satisfying soup is considered by many to be the ultimate comfort food; it certainly is for me. In fact, this might just be my all-time favorite dish of Mexico (not bad for a girl who once thought all soup came from a can!). But unlike many Mexican Americans, I didn't grow up eating it. My mom regularly cooked fideo, but always the dry version, fideo seco, or what I called "Mexican spaghetti." I remember the first time I ate fideo soup—I couldn't shovel it into my mouth fast enough and the noodles kept slipping off my spoon! For that reason, I always make my fideo soup with extra noodles, so they don't get lost in all the broth. I like to top mine with Maggi Seasoning (a deliciously salty, umami-packed sauce made from fermented wheat), avocado, and fresh lemon juice, but fresh cilantro, crumbled queso fresco, or even chopped veggies or rotisserie chicken stirred into the broth as it cooks are also great additions.

SERVES 4 TO 6

3 Roma tomatoes, roughly chopped

1 small or ½ medium white onion, roughly chopped

1 medium garlic clove, peeled but whole

3 tablespoons extra-virgin olive oil

1 (7-ounce) package fideo

2 chicken bouillon cubes

Kosher salt and freshly ground black pepper

Optional garnishes: chopped fresh cilantro, diced avocado, hot sauce, and lemon or lime wedges

In a blender, combine the tomatoes, onion, garlic, and ¼ cup water. Blend until smooth, 1 to 2 minutes. Strain through a fine-mesh sieve into a large bowl.

In a large soup pot or Dutch oven, heat the oil over medium-high heat. Add the fideo and toast, stirring often, until evenly golden brown, 2 to 3 minutes.

Carefully stir in the tomato puree (it might sputter a bit) and cook for 1 minute, just to cook off the raw taste of the onion. Crumble in the chicken bouillon and top with 6 cups water. Bring to a boil, reduce to a simmer, and cook until the pasta is tender, about 8 minutes.

Season to taste with salt and pepper and serve with optional garnishes on the side.

LENTIL SOUP
with Fideo and Roasted Eggplant

When I'm looking for something hearty, filling, and full of protein, I turn to lentils. In Mexico, lentil soup, or sopa de lentejas, is usually made with a brothy tomato base, cilantro stems, and often some cubed potatoes for extra oomph. I love this simple approach to the legume, but when I first made Yewande Komolafe's Lentil Soup with Eggplant and Orzo from the *New York Times*, it totally blew my mind. The roasted eggplant added so much texture and depth of flavor, and I'll never say no to some pasta simmered into my broth. After playing around a bit, I've married the two to make my perfect lentil soup: simple tomato broth base, cilantro, fideo pasta in place of the orzo, and that incomparable roasted eggplant on top.

SERVES 4 TO 6

1 large eggplant, cut into 1-inch pieces

¼ cup plus 3 tablespoons extra-virgin olive oil

1 teaspoon ground coriander

Kosher salt and freshly ground black pepper

½ medium yellow onion, diced

2 medium carrots, diced

1 jalapeño, minced (seeded if you want less heat)

4 large garlic cloves, minced

1 (8-ounce) can tomato sauce

1 cup dried brown lentils, rinsed and picked over

1 handful cilantro sprigs (about ¼ bunch), plus more for serving

6 cups chicken broth or water, or 3 cups My Go-To Bone Broth (page 51) diluted with 3 cups water

Preheat the oven to 425°F.

In a large bowl, toss the eggplant with ¼ cup of the olive oil and the coriander to coat it well on all sides. Season generously with salt and pepper and transfer to a large sheet pan. Roast the eggplant until nicely browned, 25 to 30 minutes, shaking the pan halfway through to make sure the eggplant browns evenly.

Meanwhile, in a large soup pot or Dutch oven, heat 2 tablespoons of the olive oil over medium heat. Add the onion and a large pinch of salt and cook, stirring often, until translucent and starting to brown, 5 to 7 minutes.

Stir in the carrots, jalapeño, and garlic and cook until fragrant, 1 to 2 minutes. Stir in the tomato sauce and cook, stirring often, until the sauce has started to thicken and coats the vegetables, 2 to 3 minutes.

Add the lentils, cilantro sprigs, and broth, and season generously with salt and pepper. Bring the mixture to a boil, reduce the heat to a simmer, partially cover, and cook until the lentils are mostly tender, about 25 minutes. Discard the cilantro sprigs.

½ cup fideo

Chopped fresh cilantro, for serving

Lime and/or lemon wedges, for squeezing

Meanwhile, in a medium skillet, heat the remaining 1 tablespoon olive oil over medium-high heat. Add the fideo and cook, stirring constantly, until evenly browned, 2 to 3 minutes.

Carefully add the fideo to the soup and cook until the noodles are tender, about 8 minutes. Taste the soup for seasoning.

Divide the soup among bowls. Top each with a large spoonful of roasted eggplant and serve with chopped cilantro and lime or lemon wedges on the side.

WHITE POZOLE

Anything with hominy is good in my book, and this pozole is no exception. There are three main types of pozole in Mexico: green, white, and red, just like the Mexican flag. The green is typically flavored with tomatillos, fresh green chiles, and often pumpkin seeds, and the red with dried chiles. The white one, which we rarely see in the States, is the most subtle in flavor and, in my opinion, the most delicious. Made by slowly simmering pork, chicken, and hominy together with little else, this recipe creates the most incredible broth you can imagine—simultaneously rich and light, I could drink it by the bowlful. A weekend soup for sure, this is so easy to make, but it does require a couple of hours of gentle, mostly unattended, simmering. I always cook a big batch because it just gets better as it sits, and it freezes well.

SERVES 8 TO 10

1 pound boneless pork shoulder, trimmed of any excess fat and cut into 2- to 3-inch chunks

1½ tablespoons kosher salt, plus more as needed

1 medium white onion, cut into quarters

6 large garlic cloves, smashed and peeled

½ bunch cilantro, rinsed and tied with twine

1 tablespoon dried Mexican oregano

2 dried bay leaves

2 chicken leg quarters (drumsticks and thighs)

2 (25-ounce) cans hominy, drained and rinsed

Optional garnishes: shredded green cabbage, sliced radish, diced avocado, chopped fresh cilantro, lime wedges, spicy salsa

In a large soup pot or Dutch oven, combine the pork, 1½ tablespoons salt, and 16 cups water and bring to a boil. Use a slotted spoon or skimmer to remove any scum or other impurities that come up to the surface.

Once boiling, add the onion, garlic, cilantro, oregano, and bay leaves. Simmer, partially covered, until you can pierce the pork with a fork but it is not falling apart, about 1 hour 30 minutes.

Add the chicken legs and hominy. Bring to a boil, then reduce to a gentle simmer, cover, and cook until the chicken is cooked through and the pork easily falls apart against the side of the pot, about 45 minutes.

Remove the chicken and pork to a large plate or platter and use a slotted spoon or tongs to fish out and discard the onion, cilantro, and bay leaves. Once the meat is cool enough to handle, use 2 forks to shred the meat, throwing away the skin and bones of the chicken and any large fatty bits of pork.

Return the shredded meat to the pot, taste for salt, and simmer for another 15 minutes, just to let all the flavors meld.

Divide among bowls and let everyone top with their favorite garnishes (I personally throw in every option on the table!).

SOPA DE LIMA

I'm a citrus fanatic. Seriously, anything with lemon or lime, sign me up. So, it's no surprise that sopa de lima—a bright citrusy soup that's popular on the Yucatán Peninsula—is one of my absolute favorites. This dish normally gets its bright kick from Yucatán limas, or sour limes, which are more fragrant than the varieties we can find in the US and have a slightly bitter aftertaste. Because I find it nearly impossible to source this specialty lime outside of Mexico, my version, made with a simple tomato-based chicken broth and infused with bay leaf, clove, and Mexican oregano, leans on regular limes for the necessary acidic brightness.

SERVES 4 TO 6

1½ pounds chicken drumsticks

1½ pounds bone-in, skin-on chicken thighs

4 cups low-sodium chicken broth, or 2 cups My Go-To Bone Broth (page 51) diluted with 2 cups water

1 medium red, white, or yellow onion, peeled and halved

1 teaspoon dried Mexican oregano

3 whole cloves

Kosher salt

2 dried bay leaves

4 large garlic cloves, unpeeled

3 medium Roma tomatoes

1 small green bell pepper, roughly chopped

2 tablespoons plus ¼ cup extra-virgin olive oil

6 corn tortillas, cut into ¼-inch-wide strips

Juice of 2 to 3 limes (¼ to ⅓ cup), plus 1 lime sliced into wheels and 1 lime cut into wedges, for serving

½ cup chopped fresh cilantro, for serving

In a medium soup pot or Dutch oven, combine the chicken pieces, chicken broth, 4 cups water (or enough to cover the chicken), half the onion, the oregano, cloves, 1 tablespoon kosher salt, and the bay leaves. Bring to a boil. Reduce the heat to a simmer and cook until the chicken is cooked through, 35 to 40 minutes.

Meanwhile, turn on the broiler and place an oven rack in the upper third of the oven. Line a small sheet pan with foil and place the garlic and tomatoes on the pan. Broil until the veggies are nicely charred, turning as needed to make sure they cook evenly, 15 to 20 minutes. Remove from the oven and set aside to cool.

Remove the chicken from the pot and place it on a large plate or baking sheet to cool slightly. Carefully strain the broth through a fine-mesh sieve and into a heatproof bowl.

Peel the tomatoes and garlic cloves and transfer them to a food processor. Roughly chop the remaining onion half and add to the processor. Add the bell pepper and process for 10 seconds or so, just until the veggies are finely chopped but not completely pureed.

In the pot used to cook the chicken, heat 2 tablespoons of the olive oil over medium heat. Add the finely chopped veggies and cook, stirring occasionally, until most of the liquid has evaporated and the mixture is starting to brown, about 5 minutes. Season with a big pinch of salt or two.

Add the strained broth, bring to a simmer, and cook for 10 minutes to meld the flavors. Remove the skin from the chicken pieces and, using your fingers or two forks, shred the meat. Discard the skin and bones (or save them for bone broth!). Add the meat to the pot and simmer for another 10 minutes to warm the chicken through.

Meanwhile, line a plate with paper towels and set near the stove. In a large skillet, heat the remaining ¼ cup oil over medium-high heat. Once hot (you can test it by throwing a tortilla strip in—if it starts to bubble, it's ready), add about half of the tortilla strips and fry, stirring often, until golden brown and crispy, 1 to 2 minutes. Use tongs or a slotted spoon to transfer them to the paper towels and season immediately with salt. Continue with the remaining tortilla strips.

Stir the lime juice into the soup and taste for seasoning.

Serve the soup topped with the tortilla strips, chopped cilantro, and thinly sliced lime wheels. Serve lime wedges on the side for squeezing.

VEGETABLE SOUP *with Squash Blossoms*

This dish is inspired by sopa de guias, a hearty and incredibly delicious soup I ate in Santa Ana Zegache, a small farming town about an hour outside the city of Oaxaca. I spent the morning with a family of corn farmers, learning about their farming methods, helping sort corn, and lending a hand in the kitchen. At first, I was surprised to see a large stockpot of soup simmering over the open flame; I'd never thought to eat soup for breakfast. But after one bite of this light yet intensely satisfying soup—brimming with vegetables all sourced from their land, including guias (squash shoots and vines), calabacita, chepil (a watercress-like herb), squash blossoms, and corn—I changed my tune.

Because chepil and guias are a little tricky to track down, my recipe highlights squash, corn, spinach, and squash blossoms. I love squash blossoms for their delicate flavor and beautiful appearance (what can I say, I like a pretty soup), but don't worry if you can't find them.

SERVES 6 TO 8

3 tablespoons extra-virgin olive oil

½ large or 1 small yellow or white onion, diced

Kosher salt and freshly ground black pepper

1 medium carrot, diced

2 celery stalks, diced

3 medium garlic cloves, minced

2 ears shucked sweet corn, cut into 1½-inch pieces

2 veggie bouillon cubes

2 medium zucchini or calabacitas, cut into 1- to ½-inch pieces

5 ounces baby spinach or 1 bunch spinach (roughly chopped)

8 squash blossoms, pistils removed and blossoms torn into large pieces

Lemon or lime wedges

In a heavy-bottomed soup pot or large Dutch oven, heat the olive oil over medium-high heat. Add the onion, season with salt and pepper, and cook, stirring often, until translucent and starting to brown, 5 to 7 minutes. Add the carrot and celery and cook until starting to soften, about 5 minutes. Stir in the garlic and cook until fragrant, about 1 minute.

Add 8 cups water and the corn, and crumble in the veggie bouillon cubes. Bring the soup up to a simmer, cover, and gently cook until the corn is tender, about 10 minutes. Taste for seasoning.

Add the zucchini, cover, and cook gently until the zucchini is starting to soften but is not quite cooked through, another 5 minutes. Stir in the spinach and squash blossoms and cook for 2 minutes, just to wilt everything. Taste again for seasoning.

Serve with lemon or lime wedges on the side.

ENSALADAS Y VERDURAS

Sides That Steal the Show

When I'm making a salad or a vegetable side, it needs to stand on its own. I want something hearty, bright, and unexpected. You know how to get people to eat more vegetables? Make them exciting and delicious! So, this chapter is full of fresh ingredients and fun flavor combinations that do just that.

Many of these dishes are not strictly Mexican. Some are inspired by my travels around the world, while others are combinations I stumbled upon in my kitchen. But because they highlight ingredients endemic to Mexico, such as corn, tomato, chiles, and avocados, or because I've given an old favorite a Mexican twist—like my Watermelon Salad with Cotija, Chile, and Lime (page 83)—they complement the other recipes in this book perfectly.

For example, the brightness of the Fresh Corn, Tomato, and Avocado Salad (page 88) goes so well with the smoky tang of my Slow Cooker Pork Ribs (page 164), and the earthy, peppery bite of the Golden Beet and Arugula Salad with Avocado, Mint, and Toasted Pepitas (page 79) tastes great with Harissa Cauliflower Steaks (page 168). It's up to you to mix and match as you like, knowing that these fun and eclectic sides will round out any Mexican spread with freshness and crunch.

CAESAR SALAD
with Crispy Quinoa "Croutons"

We often see Caesar salad on Italian or Italian American menus, but did you know that it originated in Tijuana, Baja California? Caesar Cardini—an Italian immigrant who opened Caesar's restaurant just across the California border to circumvent the US's prohibition laws—invented this salad out of necessity one night in 1924: his kitchen had been cleaned out midservice by a surprise rush of customers, so, using what he had left, he whisked together a dressing of egg yolks, lemon, garlic, Worcestershire sauce, mustard, and olive oil and served it with whole romaine lettuce leaves, croutons, and grated Parmesan cheese. The salad was an instant hit and people began to travel from far and wide to eat the famous dish at Caesar's. At least that's the story.

My hang-up has always been the croutons—they are often too big and too hard—so I came up with these crispy quinoa "croutons," which aren't really croutons at all, but just crispy quinoa that gets scattered over the salad. They're a total game changer.

SERVES 4 TO 6

1 cup cooked quinoa (see opposite), cooled

1 large garlic clove, grated or minced

2 tablespoons mayonnaise

2 tablespoons fresh lemon juice

1 teaspoon Dijon mustard

1 teaspoon anchovy paste (optional)

1 teaspoon Worcestershire sauce

6 tablespoons extra-virgin olive oil

¼ cup finely grated Parmesan cheese, plus more for serving

Kosher salt and freshly ground black pepper

1 large or 2 small heads romaine lettuce, roughly chopped

Preheat the broiler and place an oven rack in the upper third of the oven.

Arrange the quinoa on a baking sheet in a very thin layer, spreading it out as much as possible. Broil, watching it carefully and stirring as needed with a large metal spatula to make sure it cooks evenly, until very brown and crunchy but not burnt, 10 to 15 minutes. Set aside.

In a medium bowl, whisk together the garlic, mayonnaise, lemon juice, mustard, anchovy paste (if using), and Worcestershire sauce. Slowly pour in the olive oil, whisking constantly. Stir in the Parmesan. Season to taste with salt and pepper.

In a large bowl, toss the chopped romaine with about half the dressing (or to taste). Taste and add more salt and pepper if desired.

Transfer to plates or a large serving bowl or platter. Garnish with Parmesan cheese and the crispy quinoa and serve immediately with extra dressing on the side.

How to Cook Quinoa

In a medium saucepan, combine 1 cup rinsed quinoa, 1½ cups chicken broth or water, and a pinch of salt. Bring to a boil, give it a stir to make sure all the quinoa is submerged in the liquid, cover, and reduce the heat to low to maintain a very gentle simmer. Cook, undisturbed, for 15 minutes. Turn off the heat, uncover, drape a clean kitchen towel over the pan (this will help absorb some of the steam) and replace the lid. Let the quinoa sit for 5 minutes. Fluff with a fork and use immediately, or spread out on a plate or baking sheet to cool and then refrigerate for up to 5 days.

ALL THE GREEN PEAS AND BEANS SALAD

This bright and super-green salad combines blanched green beans, crisp snap peas, and raw snow peas with a little watercress, mint, and toasted almonds. I toss it all together with a mustard vinaigrette and serve it plain for a light lunch or alongside just about any main (the sharpness of the vinaigrette and freshness of the mint taste especially good with the Yucatán Snapper with Mango Salsa, page 158). If you can find hazelnut or walnut oil, it adds a lovely nutty flavor to the dressing, but you can always swap it for extra-virgin olive oil instead.

SERVES 4 TO 6

MUSTARD VINAIGRETTE

3 tablespoons white wine vinegar or champagne vinegar

1 small shallot, minced

2 teaspoons Dijon mustard

6 tablespoons extra-virgin olive oil

1 tablespoon hazelnut or walnut oil (optional)

Kosher salt and freshly ground black pepper

SALAD

Kosher salt

½ pound green beans, stemmed

¼ pound snap peas, stemmed and strings removed

¼ pound snow peas, strings removed and thinly sliced on a bias

2 medium bunches watercress

⅔ cup slivered almonds, toasted (see page 39)

¼ cup mint leaves, torn

Make the mustard vinaigrette: In a small bowl, whisk together the vinegar, shallot, and mustard. Slowly pour in the olive oil and nut oil (if using), whisking constantly until creamy. Season to taste with salt and pepper.

Prepare the salad: Set up a large bowl of ice water. Bring a medium pot of salted water to a boil. Add the green beans and cook until the water returns to a boil, about 1 minute. Use a slotted spoon or spider to remove the green beans and transfer to the prepared ice bath. Once cool, use the slotted spoon to transfer them to a clean kitchen towel to drain. Cut the green beans into 2-inch pieces.

Add more ice to the bowl of ice water if needed. Add the snap peas to the boiling water and blanch for 30 seconds; they should still be nice and crunchy. Use the slotted spoon to transfer them to the ice water bath, then drain on the kitchen towel and, using your fingers, separate them into two halves.

In a large salad bowl, combine the green beans, snap peas, snow peas, and watercress. Toss with dressing to taste (you won't need all of it). Add half of the toasted almonds and half the mint leaves. Taste, adding more salt and pepper if desired.

To serve, garnish with the rest of the almonds and mint leaves. Serve immediately with the remaining dressing on the side.

HEARTS OF PALM SALAD
with Capers, Tomatoes, and Red Onion

I love hearts of palm and could eat them out of the can like potato chips. This tender and mild vegetable is harvested from the inner core of certain palm trees and sold in cans or jars packed in water or brine. So, I was thrilled when our chef Vanessa, who cooks up amazing dishes for us when we're in Mexico, made this salad for me. The balance of flavors is spot on—creamy avocado, tangy hearts of palm, bright cherry tomatoes, and salty capers. It's such a hit and so, so easy to make.

SERVES 4 TO 6

1 (14-ounce) can hearts of palm, drained, rinsed, and cut into ½-inch rounds

½ pound large cherry tomatoes, quartered (about 1½ cups)

¼ small red onion, thinly sliced

½ cup chopped fresh cilantro

3 tablespoons capers

5 ounces baby spinach or mixed greens (about 6 cups)

1 tablespoon fresh lemon juice

1 tablespoon red wine vinegar

3 tablespoons extra-virgin olive oil

½ serrano chile, minced (seeded if you want less heat)

Kosher salt and freshly ground black pepper

1 large avocado, diced

In a serving bowl, combine the hearts of palm, cherry tomatoes, red onion, cilantro, and capers and toss together. Add the spinach, lemon juice, vinegar, olive oil, and serrano and toss to combine. Season to taste with salt and pepper and top with diced avocado.

GOLDEN BEET
AND ARUGULA SALAD
with Avocado, Mint, and Toasted Pepitas

Beets can be polarizing, but I've always loved them. When I was a kid, we grew beets in our garden, and I remember boiling them whole and eating them like apples. In fact, I almost didn't marry my husband because he's not a fan!

    Chef Eduardo (Lalo) García made me the most beautiful roasted beet, arugula, and mint salad when I visited the Xochimilco district of Mexico City—a network of waterways and island farms originally built by the Aztecs. It reminded me of my love for beets. My version includes avocado, queso fresco, and toasted pepitas, but the beets are still the star.

SERVES 4 TO 6

ROASTED BEETS
5 medium golden beets, stems trimmed off

1 tablespoon extra-virgin olive oil

Kosher salt and freshly ground black pepper

BALSAMIC LIME DRESSING
2 tablespoons fresh lime juice

1 tablespoon balsamic vinegar

1 small shallot, minced

¼ cup extra-virgin olive oil

Kosher salt and freshly ground black pepper

SALAD
4 large handfuls baby arugula

1 medium avocado, diced

¼ cup crumbled queso fresco

3 tablespoons pumpkin seeds, toasted (see page 39)

Preheat the oven to 400°F.

Roast the beets: Place the beets in a small roasting dish. Add the olive oil and 2 tablespoons water and season generously with salt and pepper. Cover the dish tightly with foil and roast until the beets are tender and can be easily pierced with a knife, 45 minutes to 1 hour. Set aside until cool enough to handle.

Use a paper towel to peel off the skin. Cut the beets into ¾-inch pieces, transfer to a medium bowl, and set aside.

Make the dressing: In a small bowl, whisk together the lime juice, vinegar, and shallot. Slowly pour in the oil, whisking constantly until creamy. Season with salt and pepper.

Assemble the salad: Toss the beets with 2 tablespoons of the dressing. Place the arugula in a large bowl and toss with dressing to taste (you likely won't need all of it). Add the beets and toss to combine.

Transfer the salad to serving plates or a platter and top with the avocado, queso fresco, and toasted pumpkin seeds.

MEXICAN STREET CORN *Two Ways*

I grew up on esquites—that magical bowl of corn kernels still hot and smoky from the grill, drenched in butter, crema, chile powder, Cotija, and a squeeze of lime juice. Any time I'd cross the border into Nuevo León I'd get myself a cup from one of the many vendors lining the streets. There's just few things that taste better.

I now make esquites and elote (all the same ingredients slathered onto corn on the cob) every summer. Elote is a great grab-and-go for parties and BBQs while esquites are fun for family dinners where I put out all the fixings like a taco bar.

ELOTES

SERVES 4 TO 6

Kosher salt

4 ears sweet corn, shucked

½ cup mayonnaise

Juice of 1 lime, plus lime wedges for serving

1 teaspoon smoked paprika

1 teaspoon ancho chile powder

Freshly ground black pepper

½ cup finely crumbled Cotija cheese

4 tablespoons salted butter, melted

Bring a large pot of salted water to a boil. Blanch the shucked corn for 2 minutes or until the kernels are just tender, then remove to a plate to cool slightly.

In a small bowl, whisk together the mayonnaise, lime juice, smoked paprika, and ancho powder and season to taste with salt and black pepper.

Using a clean kitchen towel to protect your hands, break each ear of corn in half (or use a sharp knife). Heat a grill or grill pan to medium-high and grill the corn, turning often, until nicely charred in places on all sides, about 5 minutes.

Spread the Cotija in a shallow bowl. Brush each piece of corn generously with melted butter and then the spicy mayo. Roll in the Cotija and serve on a platter with lime wedges.

ESQUITES

SERVES 4 TO 6

Follow the recipe for Elotes, but instead of cutting up the ears of corn, slice the kernels off the cob. Omit the melted butter and in a cast iron skillet, heat 3 tablespoons of butter over medium-high heat. Add the corn kernels and sauté until charred in places, 8 to 10 minutes. Transfer to a bowl and serve with spicy mayo, crumbled Cotija, and lime wedges.

WATERMELON SALAD
with Cotija, Chile, and Lime

We used to grow watermelon on my family's farm and every summer, we'd pick our harvest and sell it on the side of the road. Whatever we didn't sell we'd eat—my mom would cut it into pieces and we'd sprinkle them with a little salt and Tajín, a classic Mexican seasoning made of dried lime, chiles, and salt—I can still taste that sweet, juicy, salty, spicy bite. This salad is my fancy, grown-up version of that lasting taste memory—sweet from the watermelon, salty from the Cotija, and spicy from the Tajín.

SERVES 4 TO 6

½ mini seedless watermelon, cut into 1-inch cubes (about 6 cups; see Tip)

1 medium lime

2 tablespoons extra-virgin olive oil

¼ cup crumbled Cotija cheese

1 teaspoon Tajín, or to taste

2 tablespoons fresh cilantro leaves, roughly chopped

2 tablespoons fresh mint leaves, roughly chopped

Arrange the watermelon on a large serving platter. Grate the lime zest on top, then halve the lime and squeeze the juice over top. Drizzle with the olive oil. Top with the Cotija and Tajín, garnish with the cilantro and mint leaves, and serve immediately.

TIP: This would also be delicious with ripe heirloom tomatoes instead of the watermelon!

SHAVED CAULIFLOWER SALAD

with Candied Pecans,
Avocado, and Goat Cheese

This is my home-cooked version of a salad I ate at Nota Blu restaurant in Marbella, Spain. I've always loved cauliflower, but until I tried this dish, I never would have thought to serve it raw in a salad! I took one bite and immediately ran back to the kitchen to grill the chef about what was in it and how to re-create it at home. And it's so simple! If you don't have a mandoline, it might be worth investing in one for this dish—it makes thinly slicing the cauliflower such quick and easy work. Just watch your fingers!! I love this with the Black Bean Stew with Pork (page 52) and Portobello Mushroom Tostadas (page 94).

SERVES 4 TO 6

CANDIED PECANS

1 tablespoon grated piloncillo or lightly packed light brown sugar

⅛ teaspoon kosher salt

½ cup pecan halves

SALAD

1 small or ½ large head cauliflower, cut into large florets and finely shaved with a mandoline or sharp knife

¼ small red onion, thinly sliced

2 tablespoons fresh lemon juice, plus more to taste

¼ cup extra-virgin olive oil, plus more to taste

Kosher salt and freshly ground black pepper

1 medium avocado, finely diced

¼ cup crumbled goat cheese

Make the candied pecans: In a small bowl, stir together the sugar, salt, and 1 teaspoon water. Heat a medium nonstick skillet over medium heat and toast the pecans, stirring often, until toasted, 2 to 3 minutes (watch closely so they don't burn). Add the sugar mixture and cook, stirring constantly, until the sugar has melted and the nuts are coated in a light, sticky caramel syrup, about 1 minute. Transfer to a plate to cool, then roughly chop.

Prepare the salad: In a large bowl, toss the shaved cauliflower with the onion, lemon juice, olive oil, and salt and pepper to taste. Stir in the avocado, candied pecans, and goat cheese. Taste, season with more lemon juice, oil, salt, and pepper as needed, and serve immediately.

LOADED SWEET POTATOES

Sweet potatoes, or camote, are very popular in Mexican cuisine, but I didn't grow up eating a lot of them. As a Texan, I did grow up eating loaded baked potatoes—roasted russets cut open and slathered with butter and then stuffed with sour cream, crispy bacon, yellow cheddar cheese, and chives. It turns out they're even more delicious with camote! Something about the combo of salty bacon and slightly sweet potato is just so good. I like to serve these whole with bowls of all the fixings on the table, letting everyone slice their own little pocket and fill it with their perfect amount of butter, stringy quesillo cheese, bacon, crema, and scallion.

SERVES 4

4 large sweet potatoes

6 slices bacon

4 tablespoons unsalted butter

2 scallions, white and light-green parts only, thinly sliced

½ cup freshly grated quesillo (Oaxaca cheese), Monterey Jack, mozzarella, or queso fresco

½ cup Mexican crema

Preheat the oven to 400°F. Line a baking sheet with parchment paper.

Scrub, dry, and poke the sweet potatoes all over with a fork. Place on the lined baking sheet and bake until tender when pierced with a knife, 1 hour to 1 hour 15 minutes.

Meanwhile, line a plate with paper towels and set near the stove. Heat a large skillet over medium heat. Add the bacon (try to get it in a single layer but it's okay if the pieces overlap a bit . . . they will shrink as they cook) and fry, flipping as needed, until nice and crispy, 10 to 15 minutes. Use tongs to transfer to the paper towels to drain. When cool, either crumble with your fingers or roughly chop with a knife.

Remove the potatoes from the oven, cut a slit about halfway down the center (unless you want to have people cut them open at the table like we used to do!), and serve with the butter, scallions, bacon, cheese, and crema on the side.

FRESH CORN, TOMATO, AND AVOCADO SALAD

 This is a staple in my house because it's so easy to make and goes with just about anything. You can find amazing corn salads all over Mexico, but the Texican in me is drawn to this one's Southwest-y flair. I love to make it with raw sweet corn, but it's also great quickly boiled or grilled. Serve this as a side for tacos or BBQ or add some arugula and grilled chicken or shrimp to turn it into a satisfying main course.

SERVES 4 TO 6

3 ears sweet corn, shucked

1 cup cherry tomatoes, halved or quartered

¼ small red onion, diced (about ¼ cup)

2 tablespoons chopped fresh cilantro

½ serrano chile, minced (seeded if you want less heat)

2 tablespoons fresh lime juice

3 tablespoons extra-virgin olive oil

Kosher salt and freshly ground black pepper

1 medium avocado, diced

Set an ear of corn down flat on a cutting board and carefully holding the ear in place, use a sharp knife to slice off one side of the kernels. Transfer the kernels to a bowl and turn the corn so that the flat side is now resting on the cutting board. Continue slicing and flipping until you've cut the kernels from all four sides and have added them to the bowl.

Add the cherry tomatoes, red onion, cilantro, serrano, lime juice, and olive oil. Toss everything together and season to taste with salt and black pepper. Stir in the avocado just before serving.

Tomatoes

If you assumed tomatoes were native to Italy, you're not alone. A Neapolitan may have published the first tomato sauce recipe back in 1694, but the fruit (technically a berry—see Chiles, page 163) is endemic to the Americas. Most historians agree that the first seed was likely brought up to Mesoamerica from South America by birds, but the original tomato—a weedy plant with small, intensely flavored fruit—would be unrecognizable to us today. It was the Aztecs who, in the ninth century, cultivated the plant and turned it into the juicy and plump fruit we

all know. The Nahuatl word used to describe it was *tomatl*, which translates to "round and plump" or "fat water fruit."

The Aztecs used tomatoes in many culinary preparations, including salsas and braises, and also sliced them up plain to eat. Tomatoes remain a foundational ingredient in Mexican cuisine—you'll see them simply sliced and served as a garnish, chopped up in ceviche, stirred into eggs, in pico de gallo, or blended up with onion, garlic, and sometimes chiles to make a base for anything from sopa de fideo to birria.

Tip: If you ask for a "tomate" in Mexico, you'll probably be given a green tomato or tomatillo. *Jitomate* is the word used for a red tomato in most of the country.

TOSTADAS

The Perfect Handheld Food

I call them tostadas today, but growing up, we called them chalupas, and when I was a kid, a bean and cheese tostada was my version of a peanut butter and jelly sandwich. Both of my parents worked long hours, so my sisters and I spent a good amount of time at home on our own. We'd get back from school, starving, and look for something quick to eat. What could be easier than a smear of refried beans on a crispy tostada? Sprinkle on some shredded cheese and we had the perfect snack.

Originally from Puebla, traditional chalupas have a pinched border similar to sopes, but the ones from Northern Mexico—or South Texas—are basically the same as what the rest of Mexico calls a tostada. This is a perfect example of just how regional Mexico's food is!

Whatever you want to call them, they might just be my favorite vehicle for beans, meats, cheese, lettuce, and any other topping you can think of. I love tacos as much as the next girl, but if I had to choose between tostada night and taco night, I'd always go tostada. They're so nostalgic for me, plus so versatile and fun to make, absolutely perfect for a quick weeknight dinner or a full-blown dinner party. This chapter has all my go-to toppings plus some ceviches and an aguachile that I always serve with tostadas on the side. If you have the time and inclination to make your own fresh Tostadas (page 251), please do it! But also know that all these recipes are beyond delicious made with grocery store packaged tostadas.

CHICKEN TINGA TOSTADAS

Chicken tinga originated in the state of Puebla, whose capital city, also called Puebla, is just one and a half hours southeast of my home in Mexico City. In the United States, "chicken tinga" is often used as a catchall for any spicy shredded chicken, but a good one will always have three essential ingredients: tomato, onion, and chipotle chiles.

SERVES 8 AS AN APPETIZER OR 4 AS A MAIN

2 cups Chicken Tinga (recipe follows)

8 (5-inch) tostadas, homemade (page 251) or store-bought

Optional toppings: sliced avocado, shredded iceberg lettuce, crumbled queso fresco, chopped fresh cilantro

At least 6 hours before you want to serve, make the chicken tinga.

If making your own tostadas (highly recommended), do that shortly before serving.

Spoon the chicken tinga onto the tostadas and top with your favorite garnishes.

Chicken Tinga

I make my chicken tinga in the slow cooker (an Instant Pot or multicooker works well, too) with lots of garlic plus cumin, Mexican oregano, and bay leaf. Cooking the chicken slowly and at a gentle heat helps the flavors really penetrate the meat, plus it's so easy to throw together in the slow cooker and forget about it. Serve chicken tinga on tostadas, tacos, tamales, gorditas, just about anything.

MAKES ABOUT 5 CUPS

2 tablespoons extra-virgin olive oil
1 medium white onion, diced
4 large garlic cloves, minced
2 teaspoons dried Mexican oregano
1 teaspoon ground cumin
1 dried bay leaf
1 (7¾-ounce) can El Pato spicy tomato sauce (if you like a little more spice) or 1 (8-ounce) can regular tomato sauce
2 canned chipotle peppers in adobo sauce, roughly chopped
2 teaspoons kosher salt
Freshly ground black pepper
2 pounds boneless, skinless chicken thighs (about 8 thighs)

In a medium skillet or Dutch oven, heat the oil over medium-high heat. Add the onion and cook, stirring often, until tender and starting to brown, 5 to 7 minutes. Stir in the garlic, oregano, and cumin and cook until fragrant, about 1 minute.

Transfer the onion mixture to a slow cooker and add the bay leaf, tomato sauce, chipotle peppers, salt, and black pepper to taste. Mix everything together and add the chicken thighs. Cover and cook on low for 4 hours or until the chicken is falling-apart tender. Uncover to cool.

When cool enough to work with, transfer the chicken to a large bowl and use two forks to shred the chicken. Toss with the reserved sauce in the slow cooker and serve.

PORTOBELLO MUSHROOM TOSTADAS

I came up with this recipe years ago when I was hosting a small dinner party for friends. I wanted to make tostadas but remembered that one of my guests was vegan. Plain bean tostadas seemed too boring (though they are delicious!), so I grabbed a couple of portobello mushrooms, finely chopped them to mimic the texture of ground beef, and sautéed them with some good Spanish olive oil and a pinch of salt. It was such a hit! A little salt is all you need to bring out their natural umami flavor and meaty texture. I now make them for all my friends—vegans, vegetarians, and omnivores alike.

SERVES 8 AS AN APPETIZER OR 4 AS A MAIN

6 tablespoons extra-virgin olive oil

4 large or 8 small portobello mushroom caps (about 1 pound), finely chopped into ¼- to ½-inch pieces

Kosher salt

2 cups Refried Borracho Beans (page 242) or canned refried pinto beans, warmed

8 (5-inch) tostadas, homemade (page 251) or store-bought

Optional garnishes: shredded iceberg lettuce, chopped tomatoes, crumbled queso fresco, chopped fresh cilantro, and sliced avocado

In a large skillet, heat 3 tablespoons of the oil over medium-high heat. Add half the mushrooms, season to taste with salt, and cook, stirring often, until they've released all their liquid and are starting to brown, 5 to 7 minutes. Transfer to a bowl and repeat with the remaining 3 tablespoons oil and mushrooms.

Spread about ¼ cup of the refried beans onto each tostada, spoon over the mushrooms, and garnish with your favorite toppings!

PICADILLO TOSTADAS

This is one of my go-to dinners for Santi. I make it at least once a week because it's quick, the whole family loves it, and I always have all the ingredients in my kitchen. Picadillo, which is essentially a quick stew of ground meat and tomato, is another one of those staple Mexican dishes—someone in every household knows how to make a good one. Most nights, I simply spoon this over tostada shells, but it's also delicious stuffed into a griddled gordita (see page 145).

SERVES 8 AS AN APPETIZER OR 4 AS A MAIN

2 to 3 cups Picadillo (recipe follows)

8 (5-inch) tostadas, homemade (page 251) or store-bought

Make the picadillo as directed. If making your own tostadas, do that while the picadillo is simmering.

Spoon the picadillo onto the tostadas and serve immediately.

(continued on next page)

Picadillo

Picadillo is popular throughout Latin America, but the ingredients change a bit depending on the country. In Puerto Rico, you'll often see bell pepper and fresh recao (an herb also called culantro) added, and in Cuba, raisins and green olives typically add some sweet and salty notes. But I'm partial to this Mexican version, where ground beef is simmered with potato, peas, and carrots in a simple tomato sauce.

MAKES ABOUT 4 CUPS

1 tablespoon extra-virgin olive oil

1 pound ground beef (I like 80/20)

1 teaspoon garlic powder

1 teaspoon onion powder

Kosher salt and freshly ground black pepper

1 (8-ounce) can tomato sauce

1 small russet potato, peeled and diced (about 1 cup)

1 cup frozen peas and carrots mix (see Típ)

In a large sauté pan, heat the olive oil over medium-high heat. Add the ground beef, garlic powder, and onion powder. Season generously with salt and pepper. Cook, using a spatula or wooden spoon to break up the meat, until the beef is no longer pink and is starting to brown, 5 to 7 minutes. Move the meat over to one side of the pan and use a large spoon to remove any excess fat.

Stir in the tomato sauce, potato, and frozen peas and carrots. Cover, reduce the heat to low, and gently cook until the potatoes are tender, 25 to 30 minutes. Stir occasionally and add a little water as needed if it starts sticking to the bottom of the pan. Taste for seasoning.

TÍP: If you don't like the frozen peas and carrots mix (I love it for the ease!), you could always do ½ cup finely chopped fresh carrots and ½ cup frozen peas instead.

TUNA TOSTADAS

These days you'll find a version of this tartare-inspired tostada all over Mexico, but it wasn't long ago that local fish, like yellowfin and bluefin tuna, was hard to come by on any restaurant menu. According to my friend Gaby Cámara—pioneer of the local seafood movement and chef/owner of Mexico City's Contramar, where this iconic tuna tostada was created—many Mexicans have only recently started to embrace seafood caught off their country's own sprawling coastline. Thanks to chefs like Gaby, Gulf and Pacific Coast delicacies like blood clams, wild shrimp, bay scallops, and Mexican sea bass and snapper are finally being given the attention they deserve. Tartare might seem intimidating, but this is actually one of the simplest (and most impressive!) tostadas you can make.

SERVES 8 AS AN APPETIZER OR 4 AS A MAIN

½ cup mayonnaise

2 teaspoons adobo sauce (from a can of chipotle peppers in adobo)

1 teaspoon plus 2 tablespoons fresh lime juice (from about 2 limes)

Kosher salt and freshly ground black pepper

½ pound sashimi-grade tuna (see Típ)

2 tablespoons soy sauce

8 (5-inch) tostadas, homemade (page 251) or store-bought

2 medium avocados, thinly sliced

Flaky salt

In a small bowl, stir together the mayonnaise, adobo sauce, and 1 teaspoon of the lime juice. Season to taste with salt and pepper.

Using the sharpest knife you have, slice the tuna as thinly as possible (ideally about ⅛ inch thick) crosswise and against the grain. In a medium bowl, combine the tuna, the remaining 2 tablespoons lime juice, and the soy sauce and let sit for 5 minutes.

To assemble, evenly spread out 1 tablespoon of the chipotle mayo on each tostada. Divide the tuna slices among the tostadas and top each with a couple slices of avocado. Season the avocado with a little flaky salt and serve.

TÍP: Because the tuna is served raw, be sure to buy sushi/sashimi grade (which is usually frozen to ensure the elimination of any parasites or bacteria) and keep it refrigerated until just before serving.

WHITE FISH CEVICHE

Ceviche may be the national dish of Peru, but it's also a staple of Mexican cuisine. In this classic recipe, I quickly "cook" white fish in a mix of lemon and lime juice and toss with red onion, tomato, cilantro, and serrano chile. While Peruvian ceviche is often served with boiled or steamed choclo (a large-kernel variety of corn popular in Central and South America) and sweet potato, we Mexicans keep it simple and serve ceviche with a tostada on the side for scooping. Most firm white fish will work here, but because the citric acid of the lemons and limes doesn't technically cook it, use the freshest fish you can.

SERVES 8 AS AN
APPETIZER OR
4 AS A MAIN

1 pound mild white fish fillets, such as snapper or halibut, skinned and cut into ½-inch pieces

1 large Roma tomato, seeded and diced

¼ small red onion, minced (about ¼ cup)

3 tablespoons finely chopped fresh cilantro

½ to 1 serrano chile, minced (seeded if you want less heat)

½ cup fresh lime juice (from 3 to 4 juicy limes)

¼ cup fresh lemon juice (from 1 lemon)

1 teaspoon kosher salt

Tostadas, homemade (page 251) or store-bought, or Totopos (page 248), for serving

Hot sauce, for serving

Place the fish in a storage container or baking dish that can hold it snugly in a single or double layer (you want to make sure the fish gets submerged in the citrus juice). Add the tomato, red onion, cilantro, serrano, lime juice, lemon juice, and salt.

Toss gently to combine, cover, and place in the fridge for at least 30 minutes and up to 1½ hours.

Serve with tostadas or totopos and add hot sauce to taste.

NOPAL CEVICHE

I thought I didn't like nopales—the paddles of the prickly pear cactus—until I tried this ceviche at chef Fabian Delgado's celebrated restaurant palReal in Guadalajara. I'd always been put off by the sliminess of the plant, but Fabian showed me that by dicing and salting it, you can eliminate that divisive texture. He then tosses it with a few simple ingredients to make the cleanest yet most complex ceviche I've ever tasted. If you can't find fresh nopales, blanched green beans can be used in their place. The taste and texture won't be quite the same, but it's still a refreshing and delicious vegan ceviche. This is my simplified, home cook's version of the one he serves at the restaurant.

SERVES 8 AS AN APPETIZER OR 4 AS A MAIN

2 medium fresh nopal paddles, thorns carefully sliced off with a sharp paring knife

2 tablespoons kosher salt, plus more to taste

½ very small jicama, cut into ¼-inch dice (about 1½ cups)

1 (15-ounce) can cannellini beans, drained and rinsed

¼ cup finely chopped fresh cilantro

1 small serrano chile, minced or thinly sliced (seeded if you want less heat)

¼ cup extra-virgin olive oil

3 tablespoons fresh lime juice

1 tablespoon rice vinegar

1 tablespoon mirin

1 medium avocado, diced

Freshly ground black pepper

8 (5-inch) tostadas, homemade (page 251) or store-bought

Cut the nopales into ⅓-inch dice and toss in a bowl with the salt. Let sit for 30 minutes, stirring every 10 minutes or so.

Meanwhile, in a large bowl, combine the jicama, cannellini beans, cilantro, serrano, olive oil, lime juice, rice vinegar, and mirin.

After 30 minutes, fill the nopales bowl with cold water. Rinse the nopales in the water to help eliminate the slime (baba), drain, and repeat the process two more times.

Drain well and then add the nopales to the bowl with the jicama. Stir in the avocado, season the ceviche to taste with salt and pepper, and serve with tostadas.

La Planta de Vida

Nopales refers to both the edible paddles of the Opuntia plant, also known as prickly pear cactus, and the plant itself. Endemic to Mesoamerica, they grow wild all over Mexico. Sometimes called la planta de vida—"the plant of life"— nopales have a delicious and bright flavor. They are full of calcium and may also help treat diabetes, high cholesterol, and even a hangover! The Aztecs used their juice to treat burns and, thanks to the cactus's resilience and self-propagating nature, considered the plant sacred.

Unlike many cacti, the entire Opuntia plant is edible once its prickly thorns are removed. The paddles feature prominently in Mexican cuisine as do its fruit (known as prickly pears or tunas) and flowers. Today, you'll find nopales mixed into salads or ceviches, sautéed into eggs for breakfast, and spooned over sopes.

Nopales play a large role in the legend of the founding of the Aztec capital city of Tenochtitlán. When Huītzilōpōchtli (the Aztec god of sun and war) abandoned his sister Malinalxochitl, her son Copil confronted his uncle and was killed. From his heart, which was torn out of his chest and buried on an island in the middle of Lake Texcoco, the first nopal grew. When Huītzilōpōchtli instructed the Aztecs to build a new capital city for their expanding empire, he told them to look for this unusual plant—covered in strong thorns and beautiful red fruit—with an eagle perched on one of its paddles holding a snake in its mouth. The spot became Tenochtitlán, which grew to be the largest city in Mesoamerica and is the modern-day historic center of Mexico City.

SHRIMP AGUACHILE

I can't think of a better beach food than aguachile, or "chile water." Give me a coastal town (like Mazatlán, Sinaloa, where this dish originated) and a bowl of aguachile with tostadas and a margarita, and I'm set. I love all the variations, too—the negro with soy sauce or the rojo with red chiles—but am partial to this green one, where fresh seafood swims in a cold, bright, spicy broth of lime, cilantro, and serrano chile. This is traditionally made with raw seafood, but because it can be hard to find super-fresh shellfish, I prefer to start with cooked.

SERVES 8 AS AN APPETIZER OR 4 AS A MAIN

1 tablespoon plus 1 teaspoon kosher salt

¾ pound large shrimp, peeled and deveined

2 Persian (mini) cucumbers or ½ English cucumber

½ cup fresh lime juice (3 to 4 juicy limes)

1 medium serrano chile, roughly chopped

½ bunch fresh cilantro, roughly chopped (about 1 cup)

1 medium garlic clove, peeled but whole

¼ small red onion, thinly sliced

Tostadas, homemade (page 251) or store-bought, or Totopos (page 248), for serving

Prepare a large bowl of ice water. Fill a medium Dutch oven with 4 cups water. Add 1 tablespoon of the salt and the shrimp, set over medium-high heat, and cook, stirring occasionally, just until you see one or two small bubbles in the water (don't let it fully come to a simmer) and the shrimp are pink and just cooked through, 6 to 8 minutes from the time you turn on the flame. Drain the shrimp and transfer to the ice water bath to cool. Drain again, remove the tails, and halve lengthwise. Place in a medium bowl and refrigerate.

Cut one of the mini cucumbers (or ¼ of the English cucumber) into large chunks (you should have about ¾ cup) and transfer to a high-powered blender. Add the lime juice, serrano, cilantro, garlic, and remaining 1 teaspoon salt. Blend on high until the "chile water" is smooth, 1 to 2 minutes.

Put the shrimp in a large bowl and pour the chile water over. Cover and transfer to the fridge for at least 15 minutes and up to 1 hour so the flavors can meld. If you store for longer than 1 hour, the shrimp may start to toughen up.

Cut the remaining cucumber into thin rounds. To serve, transfer the shrimp and chile water to a large shallow bowl. Garnish with the sliced cucumber and red onion. Serve with tostadas or totopos.

FOR THE LOVE OF TORTILLAS

*Tacos, Taquitos, Enchiladas,
and Quesadillas*

This always feels like a bit of a joke to me: A taco is meat and cheese in a tortilla; a quesadilla is meat and cheese in a tortilla; and an enchilada is . . . yes, meat and cheese in a tortilla. For so many people, Mexican food is just these three ingredients combined in slightly different ways. And while this entire chapter is a collection of recipes in which meat and/or cheese are wrapped up in tortillas, they are so much more exciting than that woefully simplified description could ever suggest.

The act of rolling up food in tortillas is as old as the Aztecs and Mayans, who made a version of enchiladas by dipping tortillas in a chile paste and likely filling them with vegetables or local protein like venison or turkey. When the Spanish arrived, bringing dairy-producing livestock like goats and cows as well as European cheesemaking techniques, they added cheese and, because they weren't accustomed to spicy foods, toned down the chile in the sauces. Over centuries, the sauces, fillings, garnishes, and preparations changed and evolved from region to region—flour tortillas were introduced in the north, and chicken, pork, and beef (brought over by Spanish conquistadors) were grilled, sautéed, and stewed—resulting in the delightfully endless variety of tacos, taquitos, flautas, quesadillas, and enchiladas you can find all over Mexico today.

BAJA FISH TACOS *with Chipotle Crema*

I didn't discover fish tacos until I moved to California. Even though Corpus Christi is a seafood town, fish and shrimp tacos aren't really a thing in Texas. We mostly stick to beef. So when I moved to LA, I was delighted to discover the Baja-style fish taco, in which firm white fish is dipped in batter and quickly fried before landing in a warm tortilla that's then finished with shredded green cabbage and chipotle crema. According to some, the battering and frying technique, which is not common in the rest of Mexico and is almost identical to that used for tempura, was introduced by Japanese fishermen who came to the Baja coast in the 1950s and '60s to catch tuna. Whatever the origin, it's delicious!

SERVES 4 TO 6

Good-quality olive oil (not extra-virgin)

1¼ cups all-purpose flour

1 teaspoon ancho chile powder (optional)

1 teaspoon kosher salt, plus more for seasoning

½ teaspoon baking powder

12 ounces Mexican pilsner or sparkling water

1 pound skinless rockfish, cod, halibut, or other mild white fish fillet, cut into sticks roughly 2 x ½ inch

12 (6-inch) corn tortillas, homemade (page 247) or store-bought, warmed

Chipotle Crema (recipe follows)

For serving: shredded green cabbage, chopped fresh cilantro, and lime wedges for squeezing

Line a plate with paper towels and set near the stove. Pour ¾ inch of oil into a heavy-bottomed medium pot or Dutch oven and heat over medium heat to 350°F on an instant-read thermometer (if you dip the end of a wooden spoon into the oil and it immediately starts to bubble, it's ready).

While the oil heats up, in a medium bowl, whisk together the flour, ancho powder (if using), salt, and baking powder. Slowly whisk in the beer.

When the oil reaches 350°F and is hot but not smoking, dip a few fish pieces into the batter, letting any excess drip off, and carefully place into the hot oil, being sure not to overcrowd the pot. Working in batches and using tongs to flip, fry the fish until golden, 1 to 2 minutes per side. Remove to the paper towels and immediately sprinkle with salt.

To serve, divide the fish among the warm tortillas and garnish with chipotle crema, shredded cabbage, and fresh cilantro to taste. Serve with lime wedges on the side.

Chipotle Crema

MAKES ABOUT ½ CUP

½ cup crema Mexicana (or ⅓ cup
   mayonnaise plus 1 tablespoon
   water)
1 tablespoon adobo sauce (from
   a can of chipotle peppers in
   adobo)
1 tablespoon fresh lime juice
Kosher salt and freshly ground
   black pepper

In a small bowl, whisk
together the crema, adobo
sauce, and lime juice.
Season to taste with salt and
pepper and use right away
or refrigerate in an airtight
container for up to 1 week.

GRILLED SPICED SHRIMP TACOS

 Shrimp's natural sweetness pairs so well with the char from the grill. For even more flavor, I like to marinate shrimp with lime, cumin, onion powder, garlic powder, and a little ancho powder before grilling. The ancho adds a nice smoky flavor and gives the marinade a really nice deep red color. I serve these on small flour tortillas (like 4-inch ones) because they're my favorite, but you could certainly swap for corn.

SERVES 4 TO 6

1 pound large shrimp, peeled and deveined, tails removed

1 teaspoon ground cumin

1 teaspoon onion powder

1 teaspoon garlic powder

½ teaspoon ancho chile powder

1 teaspoon kosher salt

½ teaspoon freshly ground black pepper

2 tablespoons extra-virgin olive oil

8 small (4- to 5-inch) flour tortillas, homemade (page 244) or store-bought, warmed

For topping: shredded green cabbage, sliced avocado, chopped fresh cilantro

Chipotle Crema (page 109) or Tomatillo Salsa (page 234)

Lime wedges, for squeezing

In a medium bowl, combine the shrimp, cumin, onion powder, garlic powder, ancho powder, salt, pepper, and olive oil. Mix well to coat the shrimp, then cover and marinate in the fridge for at least 15 minutes and up to 2 hours. While the shrimp marinates, soak some bamboo skewers in water. When ready to grill, thread the shrimp onto the skewers (this is optional but makes it way easier to flip!).

Heat a grill or grill pan over medium-high heat. When hot but not smoking, add the skewers and cook until the shrimp have nice grill marks and are almost cooked through, about 2 minutes. Flip and cook until completely pink and firm, about 1 more minute.

Divide the shrimp among the tortillas and top with shredded cabbage, sliced avocado, and chopped cilantro. Drizzle with some chipotle crema or tomatillo salsa. Serve with lime wedges on the side.

Warming Tortillas

I use a lot of tortillas in my house and always warm them up the same way: Heat a comal (or a medium skillet) over medium heat, add a corn or flour tortilla and cook, flipping often, until soft and pliable. Wrap in a tortilla warmer or clean kitchen towel to keep warm.

CARNE ASADA TACOS
with Pico and Guac

Beef is king in Texas, so I grew up eating a lot of carne asada tacos. A classic Tex-Mex preparation usually involves a marinade with spices, garlic, and citrus, but when I traveled to Monterrey, Alejandro Gutiérrez—the founder of the Mexican Society of Grill Masters—showed me that all you need for really good grilled steak is some smoked salt (Alejandro gave me an amazing one, but any grocery-store smoked salt will work!) and a good cut of meat. I use this technique for my tacos made with skirt steak (called arrechera in Spanish) and serve them simply with pico de gallo and guacamole, but you could top with whatever fixings you like.

SERVES 4 TO 6

1½ pounds skirt steak

1½ teaspoons smoked salt

12 corn tortillas, homemade (page 247) or store-bought

Pico de Gallo (page 231), Raw Avocado and Tomatillo Salsa (page 235), or Chipotle Salsa (page 230)

Pickled Red Onions (page 238)

For topping: Guacamole (page 228), crumbled Cotija cheese, and chopped fresh cilantro

Lime wedges, for squeezing

Heat a grill or grill pan over medium-high heat. Season the steak generously with smoked salt and cook, flipping every 2 minutes, until the outside is charred and the inside is medium-rare, about 10 minutes. Transfer the meat to a cutting board and let rest for 5 minutes before thinly slicing against the grain.

Quickly grill the corn tortillas on both sides to warm them up. Divide the steak among the tortillas, top with the salsa of your choice, pickled onions, guacamole, Cotija, and cilantro. Serve with lime wedges on the side.

CHEESY TACOS DE FIDEO
with Chorizo

When Pepe first told me about tacos de fideo, I was like, "Wait, how do you put soup in a taco??" All I could think of was my favorite fideo soup and I couldn't imagine how the noodles would work as a taco filling! Then he took me to a restaurant that serves them: warm corn tortillas filled with fideo seco (short, thin noodles cooked in a tomato sauce) and then topped with crumbled queso fresco, chopped cilantro, and slices of avocado? Yes, my life was changed forever.

My version takes them to a whole new level of delicious, because I add chorizo to the filling and dip the tortilla in a little extra chile sauce I save from cooking the fideo filling. And then after stuffing with the fideo and chorizo and giving them a quick griddle on the comal, I sprinkle each side of the taco with cheese and cook until crispy, creating what Mexicans call a *costra*, or "crust." Believe me—these are insane.

SERVES 4 TO 6

CHILE SAUCE

2 medium dried guajillo chiles, stemmed and seeded

1 medium dried ancho chile, stemmed and seeded

2 (8-ounce) cans tomato sauce

2 large garlic cloves, roughly chopped

1 canned chipotle pepper in adobo sauce

Kosher salt and freshly ground black pepper

FILLING

1 tablespoon good-quality olive oil (not extra-virgin)

9 ounces fresh Mexican pork chorizo, casings removed

Make the chile sauce: Heat a dry comal or skillet over medium heat. Add the chiles and cook until toasted and fragrant, about 5 minutes, flipping halfway through. Transfer to a medium saucepan and cover with 2 cups water. Bring to a boil, then reduce to a simmer, and cook, partially covered, until the chiles are soft and tender, about 10 minutes.

In a high-powered blender, combine the tomato sauce, garlic, chipotle pepper, and the soaked chiles and their cooking liquid. Carefully blend, opening the vent hole in the top of the blender to allow steam to escape and covering with a kitchen towel, until smooth, 1 to 2 minutes. Season to taste with salt and pepper. Measure out 1 cup of the chile sauce and set aside for later.

Make the filling: In a large Dutch oven or sauté pan, heat the olive oil over medium heat. Add the chorizo and cook, breaking it up with a spatula or wooden spoon, until all the fat has released and the meat is starting to brown, about 5 minutes.

(continued on next page)

1 (7-ounce) package fideo

3 large garlic cloves, minced

¼ cup chopped fresh cilantro, plus more for serving

Kosher salt and freshly ground black pepper

ASSEMBLY

½ cup good-quality olive oil (not extra-virgin)

12 corn tortillas, homemade (page 247) or store-bought

2 cups grated quesillo (Oaxaca cheese), Monterey Jack, or mozzarella cheese

Optional garnishes: Mexican crema, sliced avocado, and chopped fresh cilantro

Add the fideo and garlic and cook, stirring occasionally, until the fideo starts to toast and the garlic is fragrant but not browning, 2 to 3 minutes. Stir in the chile sauce from the blender (not the reserved cup you set aside) and ½ cup water. Stir to make sure everything is combined, then leave it to gently simmer, partially covered, until the noodles are cooked through and all the liquid has been absorbed, 15 to 20 minutes. If the mixture dries out as it cooks before the noodles are cooked, add a little water as needed.

Stir in the cilantro, season to taste with salt and pepper, and set aside to cool slightly.

Assemble the tacos: Line a large baking sheet with paper towels and set near the stove. In a small skillet, heat the olive oil over medium-high heat. Add a tortilla and fry, carefully flipping with tongs, just until soft and starting to blister, about 10 seconds per side. Transfer to the paper towels to soak up any excess oil. Continue with the remaining tortillas.

Heat a comal or nonstick skillet over medium-high heat. Pour the 1 cup of reserved chile sauce into a shallow bowl. Dip a fried tortilla into the sauce so both sides are coated, transfer to a plate or cutting board, spoon in about ¼ cup of the filling, and fold in half. Carefully transfer to the hot comal and cook for 1 minute per side, until the tortilla is slightly firm and crisp. Sprinkle 1 to 2 tablespoons of cheese on the top side, flip with a large spatula, and cook for another minute or so, allowing the cheese to form a beautiful golden crust. (Make sure not to disturb the taco while the costra is forming.) When you have a nice cheese crust on the bottom, sprinkle the other side with cheese, flip, and cook until crispy, 1 more minute. Continue dipping, filling, and cooking with the remaining tortillas.

Transfer to a serving plate. Garnish with crema, sliced avocado, and chopped cilantro. Serve immediately.

FRESH-FRIED ROTISSERIE CHICKEN TACOS
with Salsa Verde and Avocado

These chicken tacos are the go-to dish in my house when nobody can decide what to have for dinner. We always have the ingredients (and if we don't have a rotisserie chicken or leftover roast chicken, it's easy enough to run out and grab!), and it's one of the few things that every single person in our household is happy to eat. Until I made this recipe, Pepe had never tried a fried corn tortilla and now he won't let me make them any other way! The technique of frying and folding takes a little practice, but once you master it, these are quick and easy to throw together. And truly—they are far superior to store-bought boxed hard-shell tacos!

SERVES 4 TO 6

2 tablespoons good-quality olive oil (not extra-virgin), plus more for frying the tortillas

12 corn tortillas, homemade (page 247) or store-bought

1 small yellow onion, halved and thinly sliced

3 cups shredded cooked white and dark meat chicken (from about ¾ rotisserie chicken)

¼ cup Tomatillo Salsa (page 234) or any store-bought salsa

Kosher salt and freshly ground black pepper

2 medium or large avocados, halved and pitted

For serving: Pico de Gallo (optional; page 231), chopped fresh cilantro, sour cream, lime wedges

Line a baking sheet with paper towels and set near the stove. Pour 1 inch of oil into a heavy-bottomed medium pot or Dutch oven and heat over medium heat to 350°F on an instant-read thermometer (if you dip the end of a wooden spoon into the oil and it immediately starts to bubble, it's ready).

Add a tortilla to the hot oil and let it gently fry for about 10 seconds to soften. Using tongs, carefully fold the tortilla over in half (still in the saucepan), making a U shape with enough of an opening to hold all of your fillings, and hold the shape for 10 more seconds, until it starts to firm up just a little. Carefully use the tongs to flip the tortilla over and fry for another 10 seconds, still gently holding with the tongs, just until the taco shell will hold its shape on its own. Transfer to the paper towels and continue with the remaining tortillas.

In a large sauté pan, heat the remaining 2 tablespoons olive oil over medium-high heat. Add the onion and cook, stirring often, until translucent and starting to brown, 5 to 7 minutes.

(continued on next page)

Stir in the chicken and tomatillo salsa, stirring to mix together. Cook for 3 to 5 minutes to warm everything through. Season to taste with salt and pepper if needed.

Scoop the avocado flesh into a medium bowl and use a fork to smash it until mostly smooth with a few chunks remaining. Season to taste with salt.

Divide the chicken filling among the taco shells and top with the smashed avocado. Serve with pico de gallo, cilantro, sour cream, and lime wedges on the side.

CHICKEN TAQUITOS

 These taquitos are so great for kids—what little one doesn't love finger food?! I keep these super simple for Santi with just chicken, but feel free to add some shredded quesillo (Oaxaca) cheese or spices like ground cumin or ancho chile powder into the mix if you like. Just to make it easy and fast, I always use rotisserie chicken, but feel free to cook your own or use leftover roast chicken.

SERVES 4 TO 6

3 cups shredded cooked white and dark meat chicken (about ¾ rotisserie chicken)

Kosher salt and freshly ground black pepper

12 corn tortillas, homemade (page 247) or store-bought

Good-quality olive oil (not extra-virgin), for deep-frying

For serving: shredded lettuce, crumbled queso fresco, Mexican crema

Guacamole (optional; page 228)

Pico de Gallo (optional; page 231)

In a food processor, pulse the chicken until the meat is very finely chopped but not mushy, about 10 seconds. Transfer to a large bowl, season to taste with salt and pepper, and use your fingers to press the mixture together, helping it stick so it isn't too crumbly.

Heat each tortilla on a comal or skillet over medium heat, flipping often until soft and pliable, and wrap in a clean kitchen towel or tortilla warmer to keep warm as you work.

Working one at a time, put about 2 tablespoons chicken filling in the bottom third of each tortilla and form it into a log. Press the filling down with your fingers to compact it a bit (this will help keep it from falling out the ends), then carefully roll the tortilla up into a little taquito. Secure the roll with a wooden toothpick and transfer to a large plate or cutting board.

Line a plate with paper towels and set near the stove. Pour ¾ inch of oil into a heavy-bottomed medium pot or Dutch oven and heat over medium heat to 350°F on an instant-read thermometer (if you dip the end of a wooden spoon into the oil and it immediately starts to bubble, it's ready).

When the oil reaches 350°F and is hot but not smoking, add as many taquitos to the pot as will fit comfortably without touching. Working in batches and using tongs to flip, cook for 2 minutes per side, until golden. Remove to the paper towels and immediately sprinkle with salt.

Remove the toothpicks and top with shredded lettuce, queso fresco, and a drizzle of Mexican crema. If desired, serve with guacamole and pico de gallo on the side.

VEGGIE-STUFFED QUESADILLAS

My friend Eitan Bernath taught me this recipe a few years back and I have been making it ever since. I usually think of quesadillas as an appetizer or a snack, but this one—stuffed to the brim with fajita-style sautéed veggies and quesillo (Oaxaca) cheese—is a full meal. When I visited Oaxaca, I got to help make quesillo, stretching the warm cow's milk curds by hand. Its salty, ooey gooey bite is perfect here, but mozzarella or Monterey Jack work, too.

SERVES 4 TO 8

3 tablespoons extra-virgin olive oil, plus more as needed

1 medium portobello mushroom, stem removed, cap thinly sliced

1 small or ½ large red onion, thinly sliced

1 small red bell pepper, thinly sliced

1 small green bell pepper, thinly sliced

1 small yellow bell pepper, thinly sliced

Kosher salt and freshly ground black pepper

1 teaspoon ground cumin

1 teaspoon garlic powder

1 teaspoon ancho chile powder

4 large (10-inch) flour tortillas, homemade (page 244) or store-bought

8 ounces quesillo (Oaxaca cheese), shredded by hand, or shredded mozzarella or Monterey Jack cheese

Guacamole (page 228)

Pico de Gallo (page 231)

In a large, preferably nonstick skillet, heat 2 tablespoons of the olive oil over medium-high heat. Add the mushroom, red onion, and all the bell peppers. Season generously with salt and black pepper. Cook, stirring often, until the liquid has evaporated and the vegetables are all tender and starting to brown, 10 to 15 minutes. Depending on the size of your pan, you may need to do this in batches.

Stir in the cumin, garlic powder, and ancho powder and cook until fragrant, about 1 minute. Turn off the heat, transfer the veggies to a large plate, and carefully wipe out the pan with a paper towel.

Set the pan back over medium heat and add about 1 tablespoon olive oil. Add a flour tortilla to the pan and sprinkle one-quarter of the quesillo cheese and one-quarter of the veggie mixture evenly across the top. Cook until the cheese is starting to melt and the tortilla is crispy, about 2 minutes. Carefully fold the tortilla in half and cook for another 10 seconds or so per side.

Transfer to a cutting board and cut into large pieces. Continue with remaining tortillas, quesillo, and vegetables, adding more oil to the pan as needed. Serve with guacamole and pico de gallo on the side.

Green at Heart

Before the Spanish exploration and conquest of Mexico in the sixteenth century, much of the Mexican diet was vegetarian and even vegan. The indigenous peoples were largely sustained by what they foraged from and cultivated on the land— often a mix of corn, beans, and squash (commonly referred to as the "three sisters"), which grow so well in that part of the world. One of the main reasons Mesoamerican civilizations thrived is because, when combined, these crops make a near-perfect diet and provide all the vitamins and nutrients necessary for optimal health. When the Spanish arrived, they brought pigs, cows, goats, and chickens, but up until then, the native diet was nearly completely plant-based. Today, Mexican cuisine incorporates much more meat, but these ancient vegetable crops like beans, squash, corn, nopales, and tomato, will forever play an essential role in the country's history and food.

TEX-MEX CHILI ENCHILADAS

I know, I know, a casserole of chili, tortillas, and shredded cheese is not what most Mexicans consider enchiladas! But these are the ones I grew up with and I'll always have a soft spot for them. My mom quickly fried corn tortillas in oil, then dipped them in a can of Wolf Brand Chili, rolled them up with yellow cheese—it's really just cheddar, but all us Texans insist on calling it yellow for some reason—covered the whole dish with more chili, and baked it in the oven until bubbling. It was always one of my favorite dinners. This recipe replaces the canned chili with homemade chili gravy, but the flavors bring me right back to my childhood.

SERVES 4 TO 6

1 tablespoon plus ½ cup good-quality olive oil (not extra-virgin)

1 pound ground beef (I like 80/20)

Kosher salt and freshly ground black pepper

½ medium yellow onion, diced

4 garlic cloves, minced

2 tablespoons ancho chile powder

1½ teaspoons ground cumin

¼ teaspoon cayenne pepper (optional)

2 tablespoons tomato paste

¼ cup all-purpose flour

3 cups beef broth or chicken stock

14 corn tortillas, homemade (page 247) or store-bought

12 ounces sharp cheddar cheese (preferably yellow!), grated

¼ small white onion, minced (about ¼ cup)

Preheat the oven to 425°F.

In a large sauté pan or Dutch oven, heat the tablespoon of olive oil over medium-high heat. Add the ground beef and season generously with salt and pepper. Cook, using a spatula or spoon to break up the meat, until the beef is no longer pink and is starting to brown, 5 to 7 minutes. Move the meat over to one side of the pan and use a large spoon to remove any excess fat (you want to leave about ¼ cup). Add the yellow onion and cook, stirring occasionally, until translucent and starting to brown, 5 to 7 minutes.

Reduce the heat to medium and stir in the garlic, ancho powder, cumin, and cayenne (if using). Cook until fragrant, about 1 minute. Add the tomato paste, stir to distribute it around the pan, and sauté for 1 minute, just to cook off the raw tomato taste. Add the flour and cook, stirring often to make sure nothing sticks or burns, until the flour has been absorbed into the meat and veggies and is no longer raw, about 1 minute.

Stir in the broth and use a wooden spoon or spatula to scrape up the bottom of the pot. Bring to a boil, reduce the heat to a simmer, and cook, stirring often, until the mixture has thickened and has the texture of a loose gravy, 10 to 15 minutes. Season to taste with salt and pepper.

(continued on next page)

Line a large baking sheet with paper towels and have near the stove. In a small skillet, heat the remaining ½ cup olive oil over medium-high heat. Add a tortilla and cook just until soft and starting to blister, 10 to 15 seconds, flipping halfway through. Remove to the paper towels to soak up any excess oil and continue with the remaining tortillas.

To assemble, evenly spread half of the beef gravy in a 9 × 13-inch baking dish. Working one at a time, place 2 to 3 tablespoons of grated cheese in the lower third of a fried tortilla and carefully roll up. Place the rolled tortilla, seam-side down, in the baking dish. Continue to stuff and roll the remaining tortillas. Spread the rest of the beef sauce over the enchiladas and top with the remaining cheese.

Bake until the cheese is melted and the sauce is bubbling, 15 to 20 minutes. Sprinkle the minced white onion over top and serve immediately.

CHICKEN ENCHILADAS
with Salsa Verde

When I moved to Mexico City, I noticed that "enchiladas" meant something very different than it had in Texas (see Tex-Mex Chili Enchiladas, page 125). The cheesy baked casserole-style dish of my youth was replaced by delicately handmade corn tortillas dipped in various salsas and rolled up with delicious fillings. There was often no cheese (certainly not any yellow cheese!) and, for the most part, they weren't baked in the oven casserole-style after being stuffed and rolled. This recipe—a nod to the original enchilada of the Aztecs—is more of that delicate style. The tortillas are fried quickly in oil and then dipped in a quick salsa verde made from fresh poblanos, serranos, and tomatillos; filled with rotisserie chicken; and topped with a little queso fresco and crema right before serving.

SERVES 4 TO 6

2 medium poblano chiles

1 pound tomatillos (about 10 medium), husked and rinsed

2 medium serrano chiles, stemmed but whole

½ large white onion

3 medium garlic cloves, peeled but whole

1 cup roughly chopped fresh cilantro (about ½ bunch)

1 tablespoon plus ½ cup good-quality olive oil (not extra-virgin)

12 corn tortillas, homemade (page 247) or store-bought

3 cups shredded cooked chicken (from about ¾ rotisserie chicken)

¾ cup crumbled queso fresco

Mexican crema, for serving

Line a baking sheet with foil. Heat the broiler to high and adjust an oven rack in the upper third of the oven. Place the poblanos on the lined baking sheet and broil, flipping with tongs as needed, until all sides are nicely charred, about 15 minutes. Transfer to a bowl, cover with plastic wrap or a clean kitchen towel, and let steam for 5 to 10 minutes.

In a medium saucepan, combine the tomatillos, serranos, onion, garlic, and cold water to cover. Bring to a boil, then reduce to a simmer and cook until the tomatillos are no longer bright green, 5 to 7 minutes.

When the poblanos are cool enough to handle, use your fingers to peel off the charred skin. Remove and discard the stems, seeds, and ribs and transfer the chiles to a blender.

Use a slotted spoon or tongs to carefully transfer the tomatillos, serranos, onion, and garlic cloves to the blender with the poblanos. Add ½ cup of the cooking liquid and the cilantro and blend until smooth, 1 to 2 minutes.

(continued on next page)

In a large sauté pan, heat the tablespoon of oil over medium-high heat. Add the tomatillo sauce and cook, stirring occasionally, until the sauce has thickened and turns a dark green, about 5 minutes. Cover to keep warm.

Line a large baking sheet with paper towels and set near the stove. In a small skillet, heat the remaining ½ cup oil over medium-high heat. Add the corn tortillas, one at a time, and cook just until soft and starting to blister, 10 to 15 seconds. Remove to the paper towels to soak up any excess oil and continue with the remaining tortillas.

Dip the tortillas, one at a time, in the salsa verde, then transfer to a large plate or cutting board. Place about 3 tablespoons of shredded chicken evenly across the lower third and carefully roll up the tortilla. Place, seam-side down, on a serving dish. Continue with the remaining tortillas.

When ready to serve, spoon over more of the salsa verde and garnish with the queso fresco and some crema.

MASA

The Heart of Mexican Cooking

Corn is a foundational pillar of Mexican cuisine and culture. Not only was it an essential crop for the Mayans and Aztecs, but it also played a huge role in their religion and mythology—so much so that they believed humans were made from corn (see Maíz, page 141). Traditional Mexican cuisine is recognized as a cultural world treasure by UNESCO because it hasn't changed that much over thousands of years, in large part due to its enduring reliance on—and reverence for—corn and especially for masa.

This one simple ingredient creates the base for everything from tortillas to quesadillas to gorditas. It stars in so many important culinary holiday traditions (what would Christmas be without tamales and a warm mug of masa-thickened atole?!) and is the basis for almost every antojito street snack sold by vendors throughout Mexico. The fun thing about masa is that once you get the hang of mixing the dough (or find a good source for buying it fresh—if you live near a tortillería, you can ask if they sell their masa), you can play around with so many different iterations.

In this chapter, I use the same base masa recipe to make sopes, gorditas, tlacoyos, and huaraches, but there are also tlayudas, memelas, tetelas, and more—all delicious masa vehicles ready to be filled and/or topped with your favorite mix of beans, meats, cheese, veggies, and salsas!

PORK AND RED CHILE TAMALES

I've never met a tamal I didn't like, but these pork ones just might be my favorite. I always add a little of the chile sauce into the masa dough for these— both because it's tradition and because it helps me tell them apart from the other flavors. I make the filling in a slow cooker—it can easily be made ahead and stored in the fridge or freezer. The dried corn husks (which are used to wrap up the tamales) can be found at Latin grocers or online.

MAKES ABOUT 32 TAMALES

PORK FILLING

4 dried guajillo chiles, stemmed and seeded

4 ancho chiles, stemmed and seeded

½ medium white onion, cut in half

4 large garlic cloves, roughly chopped

1 cup chicken broth or stock

2 teaspoons dried Mexican oregano

2 pounds boneless pork shoulder, trimmed of excess fat, meat cut into 2-inch cubes

1 tablespoon kosher salt

2 teaspoons ground cumin

2 small or 1 large dried bay leaf

Make the pork filling: In a medium saucepan, combine the chiles, onion, and enough water to cover. Bring to a simmer and cook gently until the chiles are tender, about 10 minutes. Use a slotted spoon to transfer the chiles and onion to a high-powered blender (discard the cooking water). Add the garlic, chicken broth, and oregano to the blender and blend until the sauce is smooth, 1 to 2 minutes.

Pour the chile sauce into a slow cooker or multicooker and add the pork, salt, cumin, and bay leaves. Cook on low for 10 hours or until the pork is falling-apart tender.

Uncover and set the pork in a large bowl. Shred it using two forks. Add about 1 cup of the chile sauce (you want the pork to be generously coated but not soupy) and reserve the rest for assembling the tamales. Cover the bowl with plastic and refrigerate for at least 2 hours (or up to 3 days) or freeze for up to 3 months.

Assemble the tamales: Soak the corn husks in a large bowl filled with warm water for 1 hour.

In a large bowl, combine the masa harina, baking powder, and salt. Pour in the oil, chicken broth, and ¼ cup of the reserved chile sauce from the filling. Use your hands to mix everything together and then knead in the bowl until the dough is spreadable but not soupy (it will thicken a bit as it sits), about 5 minutes. If the dough looks too dry or crumbles in your hand, add a little more broth. If it looks a little wet, add more masa harina 1 tablespoon at a time. It should be the texture of thick hummus.

40 dried corn husks

4 cups masa harina (I like the type specifically made for tamales, which is slightly coarser, but any masa harina will work), plus more as needed

1½ teaspoons baking powder

1 tablespoon kosher salt

1 cup vegetable oil or melted and cooled lard

2¾ cups chicken broth or stock, plus more as needed

Remove the corn husks from the water, shake off any extra water, and spread them out on a large kitchen towel–lined baking sheet. Working one at a time, lay the smooth side of the corn husk in your palm (if you're feeling confident) or on a cutting board (if you're still learning) facing up with the wide end facing you and the pointed end away from you. Take 2 heaping tablespoons of the masa mixture and use an offset spatula or the back of a spoon to spread it into a thin, even layer across the bottom third of the corn husk (toward the wide end, not the pointy end), making a large rectangle.

Spread 2 tablespoons of the pork filling down the middle of the masa. Bring together the two opposite long sides of the husk like a book, so the long edges meet, then fold the edges off to one side, and then back over the tamal dough to enclose. Fold the pointed end of the husk down, leaving the wide end open. Transfer the tamales to a platter or baking sheet and continue with the remaining husks, masa, and filling.

To cook, fill the bottom of a steamer pot with 1 to 2 inches of water (you can also do this in a large stockpot with an inverted bamboo or other steamer basket). Arrange the tamales in the steamer insert (or carefully leaned on the inverted steamer basket) standing upright with the folded end down and open end facing up, balancing them against each other and the edges of the pot as you build and fill in. Cover the tamales with any remaining corn husks, unfolding them and laying them flat on top. Bring the water up to a boil. Reduce the heat to medium-low, cover, and steam for 1 hour.

Carefully remove the lid and use tongs to remove a tamal from the pot. Carefully peel back the corn husk. If the masa doesn't stick to the husk, it's ready. Return it to the pot, cover, turn off the heat, and let rest for 10 minutes. If the masa does stick, fold it back up, return it to the pot, and continue cooking for 5 minutes, then check again.

Once the tamales are done, transfer to a platter and let rest for at least 5 minutes before serving.

Leftover tamales will keep in the fridge for up to 4 days and in the freezer for up to 3 months. To reheat, microwave for 3 to 5 minutes or steam for 15 to 20 minutes.

Tamales

As a kid, I couldn't understand why we only ate tamales at Christmas—they were like a present I wanted to open (and eat) year-round! Once I was old enough to join in the tamale assembly line and realized just how labor-intensive they are, it made a little more sense. But I still think they're too good to be served only once a year. I learned to make tamales from my tia Elsa, who taught my whole family how to mix the masa, make the fillings, assemble, and cook them. We did it every Christmas, chatting, gossiping, and laughing the whole time.

I now carry on that tradition, spooning, wrapping, and steaming with family and friends. It makes me feel close to my aunt Elsa and, in some special way, keeps her legacy alive. Because it's easy to source in Mexico City and Los Angeles, I usually buy fresh masa for the tamales, but I also included my relatively simple recipes for tamale dough made with masa harina. I change up some fillings year to year, but my family would revolt if these two—Pork and Red Chile Tamales (page 132) and Refried Bean and Jalapeño Tamales (page 137)—weren't always included.

Nixtamalization

Derived from the Nahuatl word *nixtamal*, nixtamalization is the process of soaking and cooking dried maize kernels in an alkaline solution (usually water and food-grade calcium hydroxide or ash), which softens the kernels and helps remove their hulls. Nixtamalized corn not only tastes better, it also makes the nutrients in the kernels more bioavailable, increases resistant starches, and reduces the presence of mycotoxins. Most freshly ground masa is nixtamalized, but you can also easily find nixtamalized masa harina these days—just look on the package to confirm. Nixtamalization is essentially the difference between delicious, flavorful, and nutritious masa and bland, boring masa!

REFRIED BEAN AND JALAPEÑO TAMALES

I remember my aunt making these when I was little, but I was always too distracted by all the meat-filled options to pay them much attention. It wasn't until I started cooking my own tamales that I realized just how amazing they are! The creamy beans and spicy, tangy pickled jalapeños go so well with the masa—they're usually the first to get polished off in my house. And if you have a batch of Refried Borracho Beans (page 242) ready to go in the fridge, the filling couldn't be easier to make.

MAKES ABOUT 32 TAMALES

BEAN FILLING
Double recipe Refried Borracho Beans (page 242) or 4 cups canned refried beans

½ cup sliced pickled jalapeños, drained and roughly chopped

ASSEMBLY
40 dried corn husks

4 cups masa harina (I like the type specifically made for tamales, which is slightly coarser, but any masa harina will work)

1½ teaspoons baking powder

1 tablespoon kosher salt

1 cup vegetable oil or melted and cooled lard

3 cups chicken or vegetable broth or stock

Make the bean filling: In a bowl, stir together the refried beans and pickled jalapeños. If your beans are still warm, place the filling in the fridge to cool for at least 30 minutes.

Assemble the tamales: Put the corn husks in a large bowl and cover with warm water. Let soak for at least 1 hour.

In a large bowl, stir together the masa harina, baking powder, and salt. Pour in the oil and chicken broth. Use your hands to mix everything together and then knead in the bowl until the dough is spreadable but not soupy (it will thicken a bit as it sits), about 5 minutes.

To fill and steam the tamales, follow the directions in Pork and Red Chile Tamales (page 132).

SOPES

I love any food I can eat while holding it in one hand and sopes might just be my favorite. These little masa cakes are the perfect self-contained package and can be piled high with whatever toppings you like and, thanks to their pinched rim, everything stays inside. I especially love them with Chicken Tinga (page 93) or spicy poblano peppers and onions, but they're delicious topped with any combination of beans, meat, cheese, and veggies.

with REFRIED BEANS, ROASTED POBLANOS, AND CARAMELIZED ONIONS

MAKES 8 SOPES

All-Purpose Masa (page 142)

2 medium poblano peppers

2 tablespoons extra-virgin olive oil, plus more for cooking the sopes

1 medium white onion, halved and thinly sliced

Kosher salt and freshly ground black pepper

1 cup Refried Borracho Beans (page 242) or canned refried beans, warmed

For topping: Mexican crema, chopped fresh cilantro, and crumbled queso fresco or Cotija

Make the masa as directed.

Line a baking sheet with foil. Heat the broiler to high and place the oven rack in the top third of the oven. Set the poblanos on the lined baking sheet and broil, turning as needed with tongs, until evenly charred, 15 to 20 minutes. Transfer to a medium bowl and cover with plastic wrap or a clean kitchen towel and let steam for 5 to 10 minutes.

Divide the masa into 8 equal portions and roll into balls (a little larger than a Ping-Pong ball). Heat a comal or cast-iron skillet over low heat. Line a tortilla press with a piece of plastic (a zip-seal storage bag or produce bag works well) cut into a long rectangle so it covers the bottom of the press and can be folded over the masa ball to cover the top of the press, too. Place a masa ball between the two plastic layers, and press down to flatten the dough into a 3¼- to 4-inch round ¼ to ½ inch thick (it will be much thicker than a tortilla!). If you don't have a tortilla press, you can use the plastic sheets and a heavy pan or baking sheet to press out the dough, trying to make sure the round is as even as possible.

Turn the heat under the comal up to medium. When hot (you should feel the warmth if you hold your hand 1 inch above the pan), carefully transfer the sope from

(continued on page 140)

the plastic liner to the palm of your hand and place on the hot comal. Continue pressing and adding as many sopes as will comfortably fit in the pan and cook until very lightly browned but not cooked through, about 3 minutes per side. Transfer to a cutting board. When the sopes are still hot but cool enough to handle, use your pointer finger and thumb to pinch the edge (similar to crimping the edges of a pie crust), making a little rim ¼ to ½ inch high to hold the fillings. Press gently in the center of the sope to flatten it a bit, then set aside until ready to use. Repeat with all the balls of masa dough.

In a medium skillet, heat the olive oil over medium-high heat. Add the onion, season with salt and black pepper, and cook, stirring often, until tender and starting to brown, 12 to 15 minutes.

While the onion cooks, peel the poblanos and remove their stems and seeds. Cut into strips ⅓ inch wide.

Add the poblano strips to the onion mixture and cook for another 2 minutes, stirring often and seasoning to taste with salt and pepper. Set aside.

Line a baking sheet with paper towels and set near the stove. Add enough oil to a comal or medium sauté pan to thinly coat the bottom (about 2 tablespoons) and set over medium-high heat. When the oil is hot but not smoking, add as many sopes as will comfortably fit in the pan and cook for 2 minutes, until lightly browned and crispy on the bottom. Carefully flip them and cook for 1 more minute, so the edges get a little color, too. Transfer to the paper towels and continue with the remaining sopes.

To serve, spread about 2 tablespoons of refried beans on each sope, then spoon some of the poblano/onion mixture on top. Top with a drizzle of crema, a sprinkling of cilantro, and some crumbled cheese and serve immediately.

(continued on page 142)

Maíz

In Mexico, corn is life. First cultivated from an ancient grass called teosinte around nine thousand years ago, corn became one of the first, and certainly one of the most important, crops throughout all of Mesoamerica. It was so fundamental to ancient civilizations like the Olmecs, Aztecs, Zapotecs, and Mayans that they worshipped the crop, each attributing it to their own god, or, in many cases, gods. According to the Mayan book of creation, the *Popol Vuh*, after two failed attempts with other materials, humans were successfully molded from corn masa. The first time, they were made of mud, but they had no souls and were washed away. The second attempt used wood, but their bodies were not strong, and they could not worship, so they were destroyed. Finally, the gods used corn and the Maya people were born.

In addition to its cultural and religious importance, corn was used as a form of medicine in pre-Columbian Mexico. Thanks to its natural antimicrobial and anti-inflammatory properties, it helped treat minor wounds, cuts, and bruises, as well as headaches. The silk, which is still used as a diuretic today, has been known to help with bladder infections, kidney stones, and blood pressure.

The ancient crop remains a cornerstone of Mexican cuisine. It is nixtamalized (see page 136) and ground into masa to make everything from tortillas to huaraches to tamales, grilled into Elotes (page 80), added to soups, and more. But because of the commercial demand for yellow corn—due to its higher oil and protein content, which is good for cattle feed—less common varieties like Velatobo, the magenta-hued variety, the multicolored Pinto, and a beautiful deep purple ear called Bolita Azul, which are often sweeter and have more tannins, are dying off. A great way to help keep these unique varieties alive is by purchasing masa from companies like Tamoa in Mexico and Masienda in the US (see Resources, page 19), which work directly with Mexican farmers growing heirloom corn varieties.

with CHICKEN TINGA

MAKES 8 SOPES

Follow the directions for making sopes on page 138, omitting the poblanos and onion. Top with 2 cups warmed Chicken Tinga (page 93). Garnish with sliced avocado, shredded iceberg lettuce, diced tomatoes, pickled red onions, crema Mexicana, and/or crumbled Cotija cheese.

All-Purpose Masa

MAKES ENOUGH FOR
8 SOPES OR GORDITAS,
4 HUARACHES,
OR 6 TLACOYOS

1½ cups masa harina, plus more
  as needed
1 teaspoon kosher salt
1⅓ cups warm water

In a medium bowl, stir together the masa harina and salt. Add the warm water and mix, using your hands, for 1 minute, until the masa has absorbed the water and is smooth, soft, and tacky, but not sticky. If you press on it with your fingers, tiny pieces may cling to your skin, but they should mostly come off clean. All masa harina is a little different, so if the mixture seems a little dry, add another tablespoon of water. If it seems wet, sprinkle in a little more masa harina. Cover with a clean damp kitchen towel and let rest for 5 minutes.

Fresh masa is made by cooking field corn in a mix of alkali and water, then grinding it and kneading it into a dough. This ancient technique dates back to pre-Columbian Mexico, when the Mayans and Aztecs would dry fresh corn, nixtamalize it (see Nixtamalization, page 136), and then grind it into a dough with a large stone tool called a metate. Making fresh masa is a time-consuming process but, thanks to masa harina (a flour made from dehydrated masa dough that just needs warm water to rehydrate it), you can quickly and easily make masa at home. Commercial masa harina, which is produced on a large scale and made from commodity corn, is available at just about any grocery store these days, but there are also a few new masa harina companies (see Resources, page 19) popping up that work with smaller farmers and use organic and/or heirloom corn to make their masa harina.

GRIDDLED GORDITAS *with Picadillo*

Gordita means "chubby" in Spanish—what a cute way to describe these dense little corn cakes—like the Mexican version of a pita pocket! Typically griddled on a comal or fried in oil, these masa patties, which are a little thicker than a typical corn tortilla, steam as they cook. The steam makes them puff up and creates a little pocket for fillings like picadillo, Chicken Tinga (page 93), and refried beans and cheese. You can also put out cheese, beans, meat, veggies, and salsas and let everyone cut open and customize their own.

MAKES 8 GORDITAS

2 cups Picadillo (page 96)

All-Purpose Masa (page 142)

Optional garnishes: sliced avocado, shredded iceberg lettuce, diced tomatoes, pickled red onions, crema Mexicana, crumbled Cotija cheese

TÍP: If you don't have a tortilla press, you can use the plastic sheets and a heavy pan or baking sheet to press out the dough.

Divide the masa into 8 even portions, roll into balls (a little larger than a Ping-Pong ball), and cover with a kitchen towel to keep from drying out. Heat a comal or cast-iron skillet over low heat. Line a tortilla press (see Típ) with a piece of plastic (a zip-seal storage bag or produce bag works well) cut into a long rectangle so it covers the bottom of the press and can be folded over the masa ball to cover the top of the press, too. Place a masa ball between the two plastic layers, and press down to flatten the dough into a round 4 to 4½ inches across and ⅛ inch thick. Getting them nice and thin helps ensure that they puff up, creating the signature pocket.

Turn the heat under the comal up to medium-high (you need the pan to be hot enough to blister the gorditas and help them puff but not so hot that they burn). When hot, carefully transfer the gordita from the plastic liner to the palm of your hand and place on the hot comal. Continue pressing and adding as many gorditas as will comfortably fit in the pan and cook for 15 seconds on each side. Flip again and cook for another minute on the first side, until golden brown in spots on the bottom. Flip again and cook for another 30 seconds to 1 minute, pressing against the edges of the gordita with a wooden spoon or spatula to encourage it to puff up in the center. Transfer to a tortilla warmer or wrap in a clean kitchen towel while you cook the remaining gorditas.

To serve, carefully cut them open on one side (don't cut all the way through, just cut a large enough slit that you can spoon in the fillings) and stuff with about ¼ cup picadillo and whatever other garnishes you like!

FRIED GORDITAS
Stuffed with Cheese and Jalapeños

 These fried gorditas are unreal. I stuff the little masa patties with a mix of cheese and pickled jalapeños, then fry until golden brown. To serve, I cut them open on one side and fill with lettuce, tomato, crema, and salsas. The mix of hot fried masa, gooey cheese, spicy jalapeño, and crunchy lettuce is sooooo good.

MAKES 8 GORDITAS

All-Purpose Masa (page 142)

Good-quality olive oil (not extra-virgin)

1 cup grated quesillo (Oaxaca cheese), Monterey Jack, or mozzarella cheese

⅓ cup sliced pickled jalapeños, drained

Optional garnishes: sliced avocado, shredded iceberg lettuce, diced tomatoes, pickled red onions, crema Mexicana, crumbled Cotija cheese

Make the masa as directed.

Divide the masa into 8 equal portions and roll each into a ball (a little larger than a Ping-Pong ball). Cover with a kitchen towel to keep from drying out.

Line a baking sheet with paper towels and set near the stove. Pour ½ inch olive oil into a deep medium sauté pan or Dutch oven and heat over medium heat to 350°F on an instant-read thermometer.

Grab one of the masa balls and make a small well in the center. Fill with about 2 tablespoons of the grated cheese and a few pickled jalapeños. Fold the masa around the filling to make a round ball, pinching the opening shut. Using your hands, pass the gordita back and forth between them while gently pressing, flattening the ball into a 3- to 4-inch disc.

When the oil reaches 350°F and is hot but not smoking (if you dip the end of a wooden spoon into the oil and it immediately starts to bubble, it's ready), add a few of the gorditas (don't crowd the pan) and gently fry until lightly brown on both sides, about 2 minutes per side. Use a slotted spoon to transfer to the paper towels. Bring the oil back up to 350°F and continue filling and frying the remaining gorditas.

To serve, eat as is or carefully cut them open on one side and stuff with avocado, lettuce, or whatever garnishes you like!

HUARACHES *with Tomatillo Salsa, White Onion, and Queso Fresco*

Huaraches get their name because they resemble the sole of the Mexican sandal. They were invented in Mexico City in the 1930s, but these days you can find them on street corners all over the country. Many vendors put the beans inside the masa dough before patting it into its signature oblong shape, but because that can get a bit fussy, I usually just spoon them on top. This simple version is garnished with salsa, onion, and crumbled Cotija, but feel free to load yours up with meats, shredded lettuce, tomato, avocado—there's no such thing as a misstep when it comes to huaraches!

MAKES 4 HUARACHES

All-Purpose Masa (page 142)

Extra-virgin olive oil

1 cup Refried Borracho Beans (page 242) or canned refried beans, warmed

½ cup Tomatillo Salsa (page 234) or your favorite store-bought salsa

¼ cup crumbled Cotija cheese, or to taste

¼ cup minced white onion, or to taste

Chopped fresh cilantro, for garnish

Make the masa as directed. Divide the masa into 4 equal portions and roll each into a ball. Cover with a kitchen towel to keep from drying out.

Heat a large comal or cast-iron skillet over low heat. Roll one of the masa balls between your palms to make a log 7 inches long. Place it between two large sheets of plastic and, using your hands, a rolling pin, a large tortilla press, or even a baking sheet, press or roll it into an oval roughly 3 × 8 inches and ¼ inch thick.

Turn the heat under the comal up to medium. When hot, carefully transfer the huarache from the plastic liner to the palm of your hand and place on the hot comal. Cook for 1 to 2 minutes per side, until very lightly browned. Remove to a plate or platter and continue with the remaining huaraches.

When ready to serve, line a plate with paper towels and set near the stove. Add enough oil to the comal to thinly coat the bottom (2 to 3 tablespoons) and set over medium-high heat. When the oil is hot but not smoking, add the huaraches, one at a time, and cook for about 1 minute per side, just until golden. Remove to the paper towels to drain off any excess oil.

To serve, spread ¼ cup of refried beans over each huarache. Spoon a couple tablespoons of salsa on top and sprinkle with Cotija and onion. Garnish with some cilantro and serve.

TLACOYOS *with Nopal Salad*

You know Huaraches (page 149)? Well, tlacoyos are the same, but different. Same masa dough but a little smaller and formed into a slightly different shape—they're a little shorter and have pointed ends instead of rounded ones. Another popular street food, these are typically filled with either fava bean puree, requesón (which is a Mexican cheese similar to ricotta), or refried beans, and often topped with a fresh nopal salad. If you can't find fresh nopales, you can substitute with jarred (just skip the salting and rinsing process) or change up the topping altogether—these little antojitos make a great base for anything creamy, spicy, or crunchy! Like shredded lettuce, avocado, and Chipotle Salsa (page 230).

MAKES 6 TLACOYOS

NOPAL SALAD

2 medium nopal paddles, thorns carefully sliced off with a sharp paring knife

Kosher salt

2 medium Roma tomatoes, finely chopped

¼ small red onion, diced (about ¼ cup)

2 tablespoons chopped fresh cilantro

1 tablespoon fresh lime juice

1 teaspoon dried Mexican oregano

TLACOYOS

All-Purpose Masa (page 142)

½ to ¾ cup Refried Borracho Beans (page 242) or canned refried beans, cooled

Make the nopal salad: Cut the nopales into ⅓-inch dice and toss in a bowl with 2 tablespoons kosher salt. Let sit for 30 minutes, stirring every 10 minutes or so. After 30 minutes, fill the nopales bowl with cold water. Rinse the nopales in the water to help eliminate the slime (baba), drain, and repeat the process two more times.

Drain the nopales well and add to a bowl along with the tomatoes, red onion, cilantro, lime juice, and Mexican oregano. Season to taste with kosher salt and set aside.

Make the tlacoyos: Make the masa as directed. Divide the masa into 6 equal portions and roll into balls. Cover with a kitchen towel to keep from drying out.

Heat a large comal or cast-iron skillet over low heat. Roll one of the masa balls between your palms to make a log 3 inches long. Line a tortilla press with a piece of plastic (a zip-seal storage bag or produce bag works well) cut into a long rectangle so it covers the bottom of the press and can be folded over the masa ball to cover the top of the press, too. Place the log between the two plastic layers, and press down to flatten the dough into an oval ¼ inch thick. If you don't have a tortilla press, you can use the plastic sheets and a heavy pan or baking sheet to press out the dough.

Carefully transfer the pressed masa to a clean work surface and spoon 1 to 2 tablespoons refried beans down the center,

making sure not to go to the edges. Fold up the sides so they meet in the center, pinching the edges closed, then shape the tips into little points. Gently press down with your hands or use a tortilla press until the tlacoyo is about ⅓ inch thick, making sure to press gently so the filling doesn't squeeze out. Repeat with the remaining masa and beans.

Turn the heat under the comal up to medium. When hot, add as many tlacoyos as will comfortably fit in the pan and cook until lightly browned in places, 3 to 4 minutes per side. Transfer to a serving plate, spoon the nopal salad on top, and serve immediately.

PLATOS

Main Dishes for Family and Friends

This chapter is a real reflection of my travels for the show *Searching for Mexico*. I thought I knew Mexican cuisine (I'm Mexican, after all!), but as I traversed the country, soaking up stories and recipes from chefs and home cooks across its thirty-two states, I learned just how nuanced and varied, complex and ingredient-driven it is. The food is steeped in history and technique passed down through families and communities, and the amazing flavor profiles of these mains, or platos, is a beautiful representation of that.

Of course, I already knew that Mexican food was so much more than tacos, quesadillas, and guacamole, but there are many dishes here that I had never even heard of! Until I traveled to Veracruz, I'd say you were crazy to pair vanilla with chicken. And I'll never forget the life-changing bowl of birria I ate after experiencing my first charreada (Mexico's version of rodeo), surrounded by modern-day charros and their families, at Lienzo charro Charros de Jalisco in Guadalajara.

Before I went on this trip, I had a few Mexican or Mexican-leaning dinners I loved to make—like the Hot Dogs el Galán (page 177) from Pepe's university days, Harissa Cauliflower Steaks (page 168), and my famous Slow Cooker Pork Ribs with Chipotle BBQ Sauce (page 164)—but most of these dishes are directly inspired by the incredible people I met and the beautiful food they were generous enough to share with me.

SHORT RIB BIRRIA

Nothing compares to a steaming bowl of well-made birria—tender meat simmered in an unctuous broth made with chiles, tomatoes, and spices—simply garnished with chopped onion, cilantro, and lime, and served with warm corn tortillas to dip into that gorgeous broth. Originally made with goat, many restaurants today offer both goat and beef birria. I opt for beef and make mine a little luxurious by using boneless short ribs, but know that chuck works equally well here, and is quite a bit cheaper.

SERVES 6 TO 8

4 dried guajillo chiles, stemmed and seeded

4 dried ancho chiles, stemmed and seeded

3 dried árbol chiles, stemmed and seeded

1 small or ½ large white onion, quartered

3 medium Roma tomatoes

4 garlic cloves, unpeeled

4 pounds boneless beef short ribs, cut into 1- to 2-inch x 2- to 3-inch pieces

Kosher salt

1 tablespoon extra-virgin olive oil

4 cups beef broth or water

2 dried bay leaves

2 tablespoons apple cider vinegar

1 teaspoon dried Mexican oregano

½ teaspoon ground cumin

½ teaspoon ground coriander

½ teaspoon black peppercorns

4 whole cloves

Corn tortillas, warmed, for serving

Preheat the oven to 325°F.

In a medium saucepan, combine all the dried chiles and add cold water to cover. Bring to a boil over high heat, then reduce to a simmer and cook until the chiles have softened, about 20 minutes. Turn off the heat and let the chiles cool in the cooking liquid.

Line a baking sheet with foil. Heat the broiler to high and place an oven rack in the upper third of the oven. Arrange the onion, whole tomatoes, and garlic cloves on the baking sheet and broil until the veggies are nicely charred, 15 to 20 minutes, turning every 5 minutes so they cook evenly. Set aside to cool.

Heat a large Dutch oven over medium-high heat. Season the beef generously with salt (about 4 teaspoons—1 teaspoon per pound) on all sides. Add the olive oil to the pot. Working in batches, add the meat and get it nicely browned on all sides, using tongs to turn often, about 15 minutes. Transfer the meat to a large plate or baking sheet while continuing to brown the rest. Once all the meat is browned, add the beef broth to the pot and cook, scraping the bottom and sides with a wooden spoon to incorporate any browned or stuck bits. Bring the broth to a simmer, about 1 minute. Reduce the heat to low.

Use a slotted spoon to remove the chiles from the pot (reserve the chile water) and place in a high-powered blender. Peel the skins from the broiled garlic and add them to the blender along with the onion, tomatoes, and 1 cup of the reserved chile water. Blend on high until the sauce is smooth, about 1 minute.

Optional garnishes: chopped
  white onion, chopped fresh
  cilantro, Chipotle Salsa
  (page 230), and lime wedges
  for squeezing

TIP: Save leftovers to
make the Birria French Dip
(page 157)!

Pour the chile sauce into the pot with the simmering
beef broth. Add the bay leaves, vinegar, oregano, cumin,
coriander, peppercorns, and cloves and season generously
with salt (you want the sauce to be well seasoned, so it gives
the meat lots of flavor!).

Add the seared short ribs and any juices that have accumulated
on the plate. Bring the sauce up to a simmer, cover the Dutch
oven, and transfer to the oven. Bake until the meat smells
amazing and easily falls apart against the side of the pot,
2½ to 3 hours.

Remove the bay leaves and serve the birria in shallow bowls
with warm corn tortillas and any garnishes.

Mexican Breads

Mexico and tortillas go hand in hand, but people often forget that many of the country's most celebrated dishes—like tortas, molletes, and pan dulces—rely on a long tradition of Mexican breadmaking. When the Spanish conquistadors arrived in the sixteenth century, they brought wheat, but it wasn't until the French occupation in the nineteenth century that many of the breads still central to Mexican cuisine were invented. Birotes (most famously used for Guadalajara's signature torta, the ahogada) and bolillos are both types of rolls inspired by the French baguette, and conchas are a direct descendent of France's buttery brioche.

BIRRIA FRENCH DIP

While the French dip is a purely American invention (two Los Angeles restaurants claim to be the original birthplace), the sandwich that inspired this one is all Mexican. I had it at a restaurant in Mexico City: a French dip with thinly sliced rib eye, mustard, caramelized onions, and Manchego cheese. One of the things I find most fascinating about traveling in Mexico is witnessing the cultural influences that remain from so many different occupations. People often forget that France occupied Mexico between 1861 and 1867 and in that brief time, they brought over a tradition of baking, and especially bread-making, that has had a lasting result on Mexico's food culture. This Mexican French dip is also a perfect example.

My play on the French dip sandwich showcases leftover birria and broth, which stands in for the classic au jus sauce. It's insanely good. If you have any leftover birria (which is rare in my house!), this sandwich comes together in about 5 minutes.

SERVES 4

4 bolillos or French sandwich rolls

4 tablespoons Dijon mustard

5 ounces Manchego cheese, thinly sliced

2 cups meat plus 2 cups broth from Short Rib Birria (page 154)

1 cup store-bought crispy fried onions

Preheat the oven to 400°F.

Cut the bolillos in half lengthwise and place them, cut-side up, on a baking sheet. Bake for 5 minutes, just to get them a little crunchy. Take out the baking sheet but leave the oven on.

Spread 1 tablespoon mustard on one side of each sandwich and top with Manchego. Top the other side with ½ cup of the birria beef. Return to the oven for 5 minutes to melt the cheese and warm the meat.

In a small saucepan, warm up the broth, then divide among four small bowls.

Remove the baking sheet from the oven, sprinkle the crispy onions over the melted cheese, close up the sandwiches, and serve with the broth on the side for dipping.

YUCATÁN SNAPPER *with Mango Salsa*

Regina Escalante, the chef of Merci in Mérida, made me the most amazing beachside meal of grilled sea bass and mango served with smashed avocado, pickled red onions, and the flakiest sea salt in the world. I sure do miss the Yucatán coastline, but my version—simply marinated fish with a sweet and spicy mango salsa—brings me right back. It's elegant on its own and even better served like Regina did, with tortillas on the side, for the most delicate fish tacos ever.

SERVES 4 TO 6

FISH

4 skinless snapper or rockfish fillets (1½ to 2 pounds total)

3 tablespoons fresh orange juice

3 tablespoons fresh lime juice (from about 2 limes)

¼ cup chopped fresh cilantro

2 garlic cloves, minced

1 teaspoon kosher salt

Freshly ground black pepper

MANGO SALSA

1 large or 2 small mangoes, cut into ¼- to ½-inch dice (about 2 cups)

¼ small red onion, finely diced (about ¼ cup)

½ serrano chile, seeded and minced

¼ cup chopped fresh cilantro

Juice of 1 large lime

Kosher salt and freshly ground black pepper

TO FINISH

1 tablespoon extra-virgin olive oil (if pan-searing), plus more as needed

Flaky salt, for garnish

Prepare the fish: Place the fish in a shallow bowl or dish so it lies flat. Add the orange juice, lime juice, cilantro, garlic, salt, and pepper to taste. Turn the fillets to coat, cover the bowl with plastic, and refrigerate for at least 20 minutes and up to 1 hour, flipping the fillets halfway through.

Make the salsa: In a bowl, stir together the mango, red onion, serrano, cilantro, and lime juice. Season to taste with salt and pepper.

To finish: You can either roast the fish or pan-sear it. If roasting, preheat the oven to 400°F and line a baking sheet with parchment paper.

Remove the fish from the marinade. If roasting, arrange the fish on the lined baking sheet, transfer to the oven, and roast until the fish flakes apart and is cooked through, about 10 minutes. Remove from the oven and set aside.

If pan-searing, heat a large nonstick sauté pan over medium-high heat. Add the olive oil, give it a swirl, then add a few pieces of fish without overcrowding (you'll likely need to sear the fish in batches). Cook for 3 to 4 minutes, until lightly browned on the bottom, then flip and cook for another 2 to 3 minutes, until the fish flakes apart and is cooked through.

Divide the fillets among plates or transfer to a serving platter. Sprinkle the fish with a little flaky salt and spoon the mango salsa on top.

CHILES EN NOGADA

Chiles en nogada—roasted poblano chiles stuffed with picadillo, topped with the creamiest walnut sauce, and sprinkled with pomegranate seeds—is considered by many to be the national dish of Mexico. I first had it shortly after moving to Mexico City in 2013 and immediately fell in love. Similar to how Mexicans always make and eat tamales for Christmas, chiles en nogada are traditionally associated with Mexico's Independence Day and only served in September. But because I'm not much of a traditionalist (and these are too good to have only one month out of the year!), we make them year-round in my house. You'll see other recipes with lots of fresh fruit in addition to the dried raisins I use here, but I'm not big on sweet foods, so I prefer this more savory version made with ground beef and pork, tomatoes, potatoes, zucchini, almonds, and a hint of cinnamon.

SERVES 6

2 tablespoons extra-virgin olive oil

½ medium white onion, finely chopped

½ pound ground beef (I like 80/20)

½ pound ground pork

Kosher salt and freshly ground black pepper

2 medium Roma tomatoes, finely chopped

1 medium Yukon Gold potato, peeled and diced (about 1 cup)

¼ teaspoon ground cinnamon (preferably Ceylon/canela)

1 medium zucchini, diced (about 1½ cups)

1 cup frozen peas and carrots mix

½ cup golden raisins

½ cup slivered almonds

6 medium poblano peppers

½ cup walnut halves

In a large sauté pan, heat the olive oil over medium-high heat. When the oil is hot, add the onion (it should sizzle) and cook until beginning to soften, 2 to 3 minutes.

Add the beef and pork and season generously with salt and pepper. Cook, using a spatula or spoon to break up the meat, until it is no longer pink and is starting to brown, 5 to 7 minutes. Move the meat over to one side of the pan and use a large spoon to remove any excess fat.

Stir in the tomatoes and diced potato. Reduce the heat to maintain a low simmer, cover, and gently cook until the tomatoes have released their juices, about 5 minutes. Stir in the cinnamon, zucchini, frozen peas and carrots, and golden raisins and season with more salt and pepper. Cover and cook, stirring often, until the potatoes are almost tender, about 20 minutes. If necessary, add a little water to keep the mixture from drying out.

Add the slivered almonds and cook until the potatoes are easily pierced with a knife, about 5 more minutes. Taste for seasoning, adding more salt and pepper if desired, and set aside.

(continued on next page)

1 cup Mexican crema or heavy cream

1 teaspoon sugar, plus more to taste

⅓ cup pomegranate seeds

Chopped fresh flat leaf parsley, for garnish

While the meat and vegetables sauté, cook the poblanos over a gas flame, using tongs to turn them occasionally, until nicely charred on all sides (this will take about 10 minutes). You can also broil them on a baking sheet in the upper third of the oven. Transfer to a heatproof bowl, cover tightly with plastic wrap, and steam for 10 minutes to help soften the skin. Carefully remove the poblanos from the bowl and use your fingers or a paring knife to remove the skin, leaving the stems on and trying not to tear the peppers. Use a sharp paring knife to cut a 2- to 3-inch slit down the center of each pepper. Set aside.

Bring a saucepan of water to a boil. Add the walnuts and blanch for 1 minute. Drain and use your fingers or a paring knife to peel off all the skin. This is a super time-consuming step! If you must skip it, you can, but your sauce will have a hint of bitterness from the skins.

Transfer the peeled walnuts to a high-powered blender and add the crema, sugar, and a generous pinch of salt. Blend the nogada until very smooth, about 1 minute, adding more sugar or salt to taste if desired.

To serve, use a soup spoon to stuff each poblano with about ½ cup of the picadillo filling. Transfer to a plate or serving platter and pour the nogada over the top. Sprinkle each poblano with pomegranate seeds and chopped parsley and serve slightly warm or at room temperature.

Chiles

It probably won't surprise you to learn that Mexico is the world's main exporter of chiles, with one million tons leaving the country each year! But did you know that all chiles in the world—yes, even Hungary's paprika and Thailand's bird's eye—are related to the original chiles endemic to South and Central America?

Most historians believe Bolivia to be the true birthplace, but chiles have been domesticated in Mexico for over eight thousand years and have played a huge role in its cuisine and culture ever since. The Mayans and Aztecs used chiles in lots of culinary preparations, including drinks, stews, pozole, and even an early version of enchiladas. They were also used as medicine for treating coughs, toothaches, and sore throats; were burned as early fumigants; and were central to many ceremonies because the spicy smoke was believed to help ward off the evil eye.

Today chiles are used in countless dishes throughout Mexico—dried and blended into salsas and sauces, used as a base for soups and stews, sliced or diced to add spice to tacos and eggs—but the types of chiles used often vary from region to region. In my kitchen, I mostly use fresh and dried chiles that are easy to find in local markets (or online). When cooking with fresh chiles, I'm often reaching for serrano and jalapeño, and when it comes to dried, I use guajillo, ancho, and chile de árbol.

If you can track them down, it is worth playing with some of the more obscure ones. Some of my favorites include the little fresh pequín chile, which packs a bright, spicy punch; dried cascabels, which have a smoky, nutty flavor; and dried moritas, which, like chipotles, are smoked jalapeños, but because they are smoked for less time, their skins stay a bit softer and they retain more of their fruity flavor.

Tip: Did you know that chiles are technically berries? Because they are produced from the ovary of a single flower and contain many seeds, chiles—along with tomatoes, cucumbers, avocados, bananas, and many other surprising fruits and veggies—are botanically fruits and subclassified as berries. And strawberries, raspberries, and blackberries aren't true berries at all!

SLOW COOKER PORK RIBS
with Chipotle BBQ Sauce

 I've said it before and I'll say it again: I love a slow cooker recipe! This is a throw-it-in-and-walk-away kinda recipe, and yes, it's a masterpiece. I've been making and perfecting these pork ribs for years because people can never get enough of them and I literally don't have to do any work! The ribs come out of the pot fall-off-the-bone tender, and the sweet and spicy chipotle BBQ sauce ties it all together.

SERVES 4 TO 6

1 large white onion, quartered

2 cups beef broth

1 (12-ounce) bottle Mexican pilsner

2 large racks baby back ribs (about 25 ribs)

Kosher salt and freshly ground black pepper

About 1 cup Chipotle BBQ Sauce (recipe follows)

Place the quartered onion in the bottom of a slow cooker along with the beef broth and beer. Season the ribs generously with salt and pepper (I use 1 teaspoon per pound of ribs), cut the racks in half, if necessary, so they fit comfortably in your slow cooker, and place on top of the onion. Cook on low for 8 hours or high for 4 hours, until the meat is super tender and falling off the bone.

Preheat the oven to 400°F.

Carefully remove the ribs from the slow cooker and transfer to a large baking dish or parchment-lined baking sheet. Slather the ribs generously on both sides with the BBQ sauce and bake until the sauce is sticky and bubbling, about 20 minutes.

Serve immediately or at room temperature.

Chipotle BBQ Sauce

The BBQ sauce is great to have on hand for the next round of
my pork ribs—or anything, really. It also freezes well!

MAKES 3 CUPS

2 tablespoons extra-virgin
   olive oil
1 small or ½ large white onion,
   diced
3 garlic cloves, minced
1 teaspoon smoked paprika
2 cups ketchup
¼ cup apple cider vinegar
3 tablespoons grated piloncillo
   or lightly packed light brown
   sugar
1 tablespoon Worcestershire
   sauce
2 canned chipotle peppers in
   adobo sauce
1 tablespoon adobo sauce from
   the can
Kosher salt and freshly ground
   black pepper

In a medium Dutch oven or deep sauté pan, heat the olive
oil over medium-high heat. Add the onion and cook until
translucent and starting to brown, stirring often, 5 to
7 minutes. Stir in the garlic and smoked paprika and cook
until fragrant, about 1 minute. Stir in the ketchup, vinegar,
brown sugar, Worcestershire sauce, chipotle peppers, adobo
sauce, and ½ cup water. Bring the mixture to a simmer, cover,
and cook, stirring often to make sure it isn't sticking to the
bottom of the pot, until the sauce has reduced and the color
has darkened slightly, about 30 minutes. Season with salt and
pepper to taste and let cool slightly.

Use an immersion blender or transfer to a high-powered
blender and blend for 1 minute, until smooth.

POLLO ASADO

Another Yucatán classic, this easy-to-make grilled chicken is my go-to for simple entertaining. The marinade, which gets its beautiful red color from achiote paste—made from annatto seeds (look for the paste in the international aisle at your grocery store or order it online)—gives the meat a ton of flavor and the fresh citrus juices help tenderize it. Spatchcocking the chicken (when you remove the backbone and press down on the breastbone so it lies flat) means the bird cooks more evenly and the skin gets nicely grilled all over. It's easy to spatchcock the chicken yourself with a good set of kitchen shears, but you can also ask your butcher to do it for you. If you don't have a grill (or don't feel like grilling), you can also roast this in a 400°F oven for 1 hour, or until the juices run clear. I usually serve this with the Caesar Salad with Crispy Quinoa "Croutons" (page 72) and Elotes (page 80)—a really winning combo.

SERVES 4 TO 6

½ cup fresh orange juice
   (from 1 to 2 oranges)

¼ cup fresh lime juice (from
   2 to 3 limes)

¼ cup fresh grapefruit juice
   (from ¼ to ½ grapefruit)

¼ cup extra-virgin olive oil

4 garlic cloves, minced or
   grated

2 tablespoons crumbled
   achiote paste

Kosher salt

2 teaspoons dried Mexican
   oregano

1 teaspoon ground cumin

⅛ teaspoon ground cloves

1 whole chicken (about
   4 pounds), spatchcocked

In a bowl or baking dish that will comfortably hold the chicken, whisk together the orange juice, lime juice, grapefruit juice, olive oil, garlic, achiote paste, salt (I use 1 teaspoon per pound of meat), oregano, cumin, and cloves. Add the chicken, turning it over to coat evenly, then cover the bowl with plastic wrap and marinate for at least 2 hours and up to 8 hours, turning halfway through.

Heat a charcoal or gas grill to medium-low (if using a charcoal grill, you may want to bank your coals to one side and cook the chicken over indirect heat). Set the chicken on the grate skin-side down and grill, with the lid closed, for 50 minutes to 1 hour (or until a thermometer inserted into the leg/thigh joint registers 165°F), flipping every 15 minutes so the skin gets nice and crispy and the chicken cooks evenly.

Transfer to a carving board and tent with foil. Let rest for at least 10 minutes before carving and serving.

HARISSA CAULIFLOWER STEAKS

I've gone through my own phases of veganism or vegetarianism and have lots of friends who abstain from eating animal protein, so I'm always looking for satisfying plant-based mains to add to my arsenal. I love cutting into this thick, spicy cauliflower steak, but it almost didn't make it into the book. I wasn't sure that anything slathered in harissa—a spice paste that comes from the Maghreb region of Africa—worked in a cookbook about Mexican food. But when I investigated the history, I learned that the chiles used for Tunisian harissa were likely brought to that part of the world via Mexico in the 1600s, when the Spanish occupied Ottoman Tunisia. Yet another example of how colonization has influenced and shaped food traditions around the world for centuries!

SERVES 4 TO 6

2 medium heads cauliflower

¼ cup Harissa (recipe follows)

¼ cup extra-virgin olive oil

Kosher salt and freshly ground black pepper

Chopped fresh cilantro, for garnish

Preheat the oven to 425°F. Line a baking sheet with parchment paper.

Set the cauliflower stem-side up and cut down through the core into ¾-inch "steaks." Place the cauliflower steaks (and any extra florets if you want to roast them, too) in a large bowl or baking dish and toss with the harissa and olive oil, using your fingers to spread the paste evenly over all the cauliflower pieces.

Arrange the steaks on the lined baking sheet, season each one with a little salt and pepper, and roast, flipping halfway through, until the cauliflower is super crispy around the edges and easily pierced with a sharp knife, 25 to 30 minutes.

Remove from the oven, arrange on a serving platter, and garnish with chopped cilantro.

Harissa

MAKES ABOUT 1¼ CUPS

3 dried guajillo chiles, stemmed
  and seeded
1 dried ancho chile, stemmed
  and seeded
1 dried árbol chile, stemmed
  and seeded
3 garlic cloves, roughly chopped
2 tablespoons fresh lemon juice
1 tablespoon tomato paste
1 teaspoon ground cumin
1 teaspoon ground coriander
1 teaspoon smoked paprika
⅓ cup extra-virgin olive oil
Kosher salt and freshly ground
  black pepper

Heat a large comal or cast-iron skillet over medium heat. Add the chiles and cook until toasted and fragrant, about 5 minutes, flipping halfway through. Transfer to a small saucepan, add water to cover, and bring to a boil. Turn off the heat, cover, and let sit for 15 minutes.

Drain the soaked chiles and transfer to a food processor. Add the garlic, lemon juice, tomato paste, cumin, coriander, and smoked paprika. Blend until the chiles have started to break down, about 10 seconds. With the food processor running, drizzle in the olive oil in a slow stream and continue blending until the harissa is smooth. Season to taste with salt and pepper and transfer to a jar.

SLOW-COOKED PORK BELLY
with Beet Puree, Watercress,
and Pickled Red Onions

I'm not a huge pork eater, but I will never turn down a nice, crispy piece of pork belly. This dish is inspired by one I had at Ixi'im, a stunning restaurant in the city of Chocholá on the Yucatán Peninsula, run by chef Luis Ronzón. Luis served me the prettiest plate of pork belly I've ever seen—garnished with pickled carrots and purslane and served alongside multiple sauces and salsas for dipping. Because this was the Yucatán, his pork was cooked in a píib (a traditional earthen oven used throughout the region), but I cook mine low and slow in the oven to achieve similarly tender results (and note that you do need to let it rest in the fridge overnight with its salt and sugar dry rub). After a quick sizzle in a hot pan, you have the crispiest, most succulent pork belly you can imagine. I serve it with the earthy beet sauce I learned from Luis, plus pickled red onions and watercress (with warm corn tortillas on the side, of course!), but this pork would be delicious on just about anything.

2½-pound piece pork belly, skin removed but with a nice layer of fat on top

Kosher salt

1 teaspoon grated piloncillo or lightly packed light brown sugar

3 medium beets, unpeeled

1 tablespoon extra-virgin olive oil

Freshly ground black pepper

2 tablespoons unsalted butter, cubed

1 bunch watercress

Pickled Red Onions (page 238)

Lemon wedges, for squeezing

Place the pork belly in a baking dish that can hold it snugly. In a small bowl, combine 1 tablespoon plus 1 teaspoon kosher salt and the brown sugar and rub the mixture all over the meat. Cover with plastic wrap and put in the fridge overnight (at least 8 hours and up to 24).

Preheat the oven to 300°F.

Pull the pork out of the fridge, wipe out any liquid that has accumulated in the dish, and pat the pork belly dry. Return the pork belly to the baking dish, cover tightly with foil, transfer to the oven, and cook until easily pierced with a knife but not falling apart, about 3 hours. Once cooked, carefully transfer to a plate to cool slightly.

At the same time the pork is in the oven, scrub the beets well and place them in a small baking dish. Toss with the olive oil, season generously with salt and pepper, and cover tightly with foil. Transfer to the oven and roast until tender when pierced with a fork, 1½ to 2 hours.

Remove the beets and, when cool enough to handle, use a clean kitchen towel or paper towel to peel off the skin. Roughly chop and transfer to a high-powered blender along with the butter and 2 tablespoons water. Blend on high, adding more water as needed, until smooth, 1 to 2 minutes. Season to taste with salt and pepper.

Heat a large sauté pan over medium heat. When the pan is hot, add the pork belly, fat-side down, and cook, using a spatula to press down to make sure it cooks evenly, until the fat is crispy and golden, 3 to 4 minutes. Turn and cook the bottom until crisp and browned, about 2 minutes.

Transfer to a cutting board and cut the pork into ¼- to ½-inch slices (if you're eating this in tacos you may want to cut the piece in half lengthwise first, then into slices, so the pieces are more bite-size). Serve on a platter with the watercress, bowls of pickled red onions, and the beet puree, with lemon wedges on the side for squeezing.

STUFFED CALABACITA BOATS

Growing up on a working ranch, we ate whatever we grew. This meant that, during calabacita season, we ate A LOT of calabacita. To keep us from getting too bored, my mom would get creative, coming up with dozens of different ways to cook the squash. Some of her experiments were, erm, a little more successful than others, but this recipe was always a hit. It made dinner so fun! My sisters and I would pick up the little boats with our hands and play with them at the table, which helped distract us from the fact that we'd already eaten squash six times that week.

SERVES 4 TO 6

2 tablespoons extra-virgin olive oil

½ small white onion, diced

2 medium garlic cloves, minced

½ pound ground beef (I like 80/20) or ground turkey for a leaner option

1 tablespoon Italian seasoning

Kosher salt and freshly ground black pepper

1 tablespoon tomato paste

1 (14.5-ounce) can diced tomatoes, undrained

6 large calabacitas (stem-on, preferably) or 4 large zucchini

¼ cup grated Parmesan cheese

Preheat the oven to 375°F.

In a large sauté pan or Dutch oven, heat the oil over medium-high heat. Add the onion and cook until translucent and starting to brown, 5 to 7 minutes. Stir in the garlic and cook until fragrant and starting to brown, about 2 minutes.

Add the ground beef and Italian seasoning. Season generously with salt and pepper and cook, breaking the meat up with a spatula, until no longer pink, 5 to 7 minutes. Move the meat and veggies over to one side of the pan and use a large spoon to remove any excess fat. Add the tomato paste, stir it around in the pan, and cook for 1 minute to cook off the raw tomato taste.

Add the diced tomatoes and their juices and give the sauce a good stir. Reduce the heat to maintain a gentle simmer and cook until the sauce has thickened and is no longer soupy, about 20 minutes. Taste for seasoning, adding more salt and pepper if desired.

Cut the squash (stems on) down the middle lengthwise and use a teaspoon to carefully scrape out the seeds and soft core. Season each "boat" with a little salt and pepper and place in a large baking dish or on a baking sheet.

Carefully spoon the mixture into the squash boats and top with the Parmesan. Bake until the squash is tender when pierced with a paring knife, 20 to 25 minutes.

VANILLA CHICKEN

I think the forbidden fruit in the garden of Eden should have been a vanilla bean. If you ask me, this romantic, rare, beautifully scented orchid would have been a much more compelling temptation for Eve! I already put vanilla in every sweet dish and drink I can think of, so when Norma Gaya—who runs her family's vanilla plantation Gaya Vai-Mex in Veracruz—showed me how to make this vanilla chicken, I was seriously excited. Vanilla with savory food?! It opened a whole new world of possibilities for me. If you're skeptical, give this dish a try. Just one bite of this tender chicken, swimming in a rich, vanilla cream sauce, is sure to change your mind.

SERVES 4 TO 6

2 pounds boneless, skinless chicken thighs (about 8), cut into 2-inch pieces

½ cup apple cider vinegar

Kosher salt and freshly ground black pepper

7 tablespoons unsalted butter

1 medium white onion, halved and thinly sliced

1 vanilla bean

1 cup whole milk

2 cups heavy cream

2 tablespoons vanilla extract (preferably Mexican)

12 corn tortillas, homemade (page 247) or store-bought, warmed

In a large bowl, combine the chicken thighs and vinegar and season generously with salt and pepper.

In a large sauté pan or Dutch oven, heat 3 tablespoons of the butter over medium heat. When the butter has melted, add the onion and season with salt and pepper. Cook, stirring often, until tender and just starting to brown, 7 to 10 minutes. Transfer to a high-powered blender.

Cut the vanilla bean open lengthwise and use a paring knife to carefully scrape out the seeds into the blender. Add the milk, cream, and vanilla extract and blend until the sauce has thickened and is mostly smooth, 20 to 30 seconds. Season with salt and pepper to taste.

In the same sauté pan, heat the remaining 4 tablespoons butter over medium heat. Drain the chicken pieces and add them to the pan. Stir in the vanilla sauce, add the scraped out vanilla pod, and bring the mixture to a low simmer. Cook gently, stirring occasionally, until the chicken is cooked through and the sauce has thickened slightly, 30 to 40 minutes.

Transfer the chicken to serving plates or a large serving platter, leaving much of the sauce behind in the pot. Using tongs, dip the warm tortillas in the sauce on both sides and place alongside the chicken. Spoon a little more sauce over everything and serve immediately.

HOT DOGS EL GALÁN

El galán means "good looking" or "dreamboat" in Spanish and these are certainly the best-looking hot dogs I've ever had! I learned to make this dish for my husband, who has fond memories of eating them in his youth in Mexico City. According to Pepe, there was a very famous hot dog vendor who would set up shop outside one of the popular nightclubs. He and his friends would come out, probably a little tipsy from a night of drinking, and inhale these hot dogs, which were smothered in the most addictive sauce you can imagine. A mix of bacon, onion, tomato, pickled jalapeño, mustard, ketchup, and cheese, this sauce is my secret weapon not just for hot dogs, but also eggs, burgers, beans . . . anything!

SERVES 4 TO 8

1 (8-ounce) package bacon (7 slices)

1 medium yellow onion, diced

2 Roma tomatoes, diced

⅓ cup pickled jalapeños, drained and finely chopped

¼ cup yellow mustard

½ cup ketchup

8 hot dogs or turkey dogs

8 hot dog buns

Butter, for the buns (optional)

1 cup shredded cheddar or Mexican blend cheese

Line a plate with paper towels and set near the stove. Heat a large sauté pan over medium heat. Add the bacon (try to get it in a single layer but it's okay if the pieces overlap a bit . . . they will shrink as they cook) and fry, flipping as needed, until nice and crispy, 10 to 15 minutes. Use tongs to transfer to the paper towels. Turn off the heat.

Carefully pour off all but 2 tablespoons of the bacon fat (reserve it for Refried Borracho Beans, page 242!). Set the pan over medium heat, add the onion and tomatoes, and cook until the liquid from the tomatoes has cooked off and the onion is tender, 7 to 10 minutes.

Meanwhile, roughly chop up the cooled bacon and set aside.

Add the jalapeños, mustard, and ketchup to the onion mixture and cook for another minute until warmed through.

Cook the hot dogs (I like mine boiled and then grilled) and toast the buns (I highly recommend buttering your buns before toasting or grilling!).

Just before serving, stir the chopped-up bacon and shredded cheese into the ketchupy onion mixture. Add the hot dogs to the buns, and top each with a few generous spoonfuls of sauce and serve.

POSTRES

A Sweet Finish

Have you noticed that so many great cooks steer clear of desserts? I think it's because baking has a reputation for being so specific, so . . . scientific. My favorite part about cooking is improvising, using what I have, and making it up as I go—the last thing I want is to worry about mismeasuring a tablespoon of this or a teaspoon of that and ruining a whole cake! But a dessert doesn't have to be complicated or preciously precise to be delicious. In fact, many of the most popular desserts in Mexico like Paletas (page 198) and Carlota de Limón (page 184) are perfect for more instinctual cooks like me. Maybe it's because Mexican recipes (both sweet and savory) are often passed down through generations and as such, are based on feel, sight, and smell, rather than exact measurements. But if you don't have the benefit of generations of taste memory and an abuela to make Buñuelos (page 187) with you, a recipe—with measurements, yes!—is your next best bet.

This chapter is full of simple yet undeniably impressive desserts I turn to again and again. These sweet treats are super flexible and forgiving while still delivering on texture, flavor, and wow factor. Love bananas? Add more to the flambé! Don't have time to make ice cream? Buy some from the store! And the recipes that do require measuring spoons are well worth the extra effort. Just wait until you invert that Chocoflan (page 192), often called the impossible cake because its flan and chocolate cake layers switch places while baking . . . your friends and family will go wild!

TRES LECHES CAKE

Tres leches cake (thus named because the simple sponge base is soaked in a mix of three milks: sweetened condensed milk, evaporated milk, and whole milk or heavy cream) is ubiquitous in Mexico, and is popular all over Latin America. There's a lively debate about whether the first version was made in Mexico or Nicaragua—I don't know the answer to this, but I do know you can find it in just about any Mexican bakery. It's simple to make and especially great during hot months when you want something cool and refreshing and don't want to worry about buttercream melting! I bake my cake the morning of a dinner party or celebration so it has all day to soak up that cold, sweet, milky mixture.

SERVES 12

Softened unsalted butter, for the pan

1⅔ cups cake flour

1½ teaspoons baking powder

½ teaspoon kosher salt

5 large eggs, separated

1 cup sugar

¼ cup whole milk

1 tablespoon vanilla extract (preferably Mexican)

1 (12-ounce) can evaporated milk

1 (14-ounce) can sweetened condensed milk

1 cup heavy cream

WHIPPED CREAM
2 cups heavy cream

Sugar

2 teaspoons vanilla extract (preferably Mexican)

Preheat the oven to 350°F. Generously butter a 9 × 13-inch baking dish.

In a medium bowl, whisk together the flour, baking powder, and salt.

In a stand mixer fitted with the whisk, beat the egg whites on medium speed until soft peaks form, 2 to 3 minutes. With the machine running, slowly sprinkle in the sugar. Scrape down the sides of the bowl with a spatula to make sure all the sugar has been mixed in, increase the speed to medium-high, and whisk until stiff peaks form (like a meringue), another 3 to 4 minutes. Reduce the speed to medium and add the yolks, one at a time, whisking thoroughly after each addition. Add the milk and vanilla and whisk again just to combine.

Remove the bowl from the mixer and use a spatula to gently fold in the flour mixture a little at a time, trying not to deflate the whipped eggs too much. Transfer the batter to the prepared baking dish and use a spatula to spread it out evenly in the pan.

Bake until the top is golden brown, the cake doesn't jiggle at all in the center when you shake it, and a toothpick inserted into the center comes out clean (or with just a crumb or two

(continued on page 182)

attached), 28 to 30 minutes. Set the baking dish on a cooling rack and let cool completely.

Once the cake is cooled, in a medium bowl, whisk together the evaporated milk, sweetened condensed milk, and heavy cream. Poke the cake all over with a toothpick or wooden skewer and pour the milk mixture, a little at a time to let it soak in, over the top. Cover the pan with plastic wrap or foil and refrigerate for at least 3 hours or preferably overnight.

Make the whipped cream: Before serving, in a stand mixer fitted with the whisk, whip the cream until it holds soft peaks, adding sugar to taste (the cake itself is very sweet so I like to go light on the sugar here) and the vanilla.

Spread the whipped cream evenly over the top of the cake and cut into squares to serve. Store in the fridge, covered with plastic wrap or in an airtight container, for up to 3 days.

The Truth About Fake Vanilla

Vanilla is one of the most labor-intensive crops in the world—the entire process of growing, hand-pollinating, and curing a vanilla bean takes about one year, and each flower will only produce one pod! As a result, vanilla is one of the most expensive food items, second only to saffron.

Because of this, much of the vanilla extract available to consumers is made with artificial flavors—in fact, 95 percent of the vanilla extract available for purchase is synthetic. It's hard not to balk at the price of vanilla in the grocery store at first, but if you could see the painstaking work required to produce each individual bean, you'd understand why. If you can afford it, check the labels and look for extracts that contain only vanilla and alcohol. And try to seek out Mexican vanilla—you'll be supporting a centuries-old tradition of vanilla farming in the plant's original birthplace (see Vanilla, the Edible Orchid, page 40).

BANANAS FLAMBÉS
with Vanilla Liqueur

I ate a version of this wonderfully simple, yet undeniably delicious dessert at my friend Norma Gaya's family home after a day spent filming *Searching for Mexico* in their vanilla fields in the mountains of Veracruz. I just love how the cold vanilla bean ice cream melts into the hot bananas and buttery caramel sauce. I also love how quick and easy it is to make! So many people are intimidated by flambéing . . . don't be! It's actually super simple and so impressive. I always use a long stick lighter but a long match works well, too. Don't forget the pinch of flaky salt just before serving—it helps balance the different layers of sweetness in the dish.

SERVES 4 TO 6

4 tablespoons unsalted butter

¼ cup grated piloncillo or packed light brown sugar

4 large firm-ripe bananas, cut into ½-inch slices

¼ cup vanilla liqueur, such as Xanath by the Gaya family, or rum

Flaky salt

Vanilla bean ice cream

In a large nonstick sauté pan, heat the butter over medium heat. Once the butter is melted, stir in the brown sugar and cook, stirring often, until the sugar has dissolved and the mixture smells nutty, about 2 minutes. Add the bananas, gently stir to coat them in the caramel, and cook for 1 minute just to soften.

Turn off the heat and add the vanilla liqueur. If flambéing, use a long stick lighter or a long match to ignite the alcohol, let the flames burn off, then serve. (If skipping the flambé step, turn the heat back on and simmer for 2 to 3 minutes, until the alcohol has cooked off and the sauce has thickened.)

Divide among serving dishes and top each portion with a sprinkle of flaky salt and a scoop of vanilla ice cream.

CARLOTA DE LIMÓN

Any dessert with citrus is my jam. I love a key lime pie, but I rarely have the time or the energy to make one from scratch. When I discovered Carlota de Limón—essentially an icebox cake (read: easiest dessert ever) with all the flavors of key lime pie—I was over the moon. The hardest part about this dessert will be tracking down the Maria cookies (a mild, not overly sweet biscuit popular in countries throughout Latin America), but any Latin grocer and lots of large chain stores stock them, or you can find them online. Do keep in mind that this cake needs to chill for at least 8 hours before serving.

SERVES 12

- 1 (12-ounce) can evaporated milk
- 1 (14-ounce) can sweetened condensed milk
- ½ cup fresh lime juice (from 4 to 6 limes)
- 2 tablespoons fresh lemon juice
- 1 (7-ounce) package Maria cookies
- Grated zest of 1 lime

Pour the evaporated milk and sweetened condensed milk into a high-powered blender and blend for 10 seconds, just to combine. Add the lime juice and lemon juice and blend again until the mixture thickens and is smooth, another 10 seconds or so.

Open the package of cookies and reserve 6 for the top of the cake. In an 8-inch square or round baking dish, add one-quarter of the cream mixture (about 1 cup) and arrange 11 cookies (one-third of the remaining package) on top, breaking them as needed to fit in a single layer. Repeat with two more layers of cream and cookies. Top with a final layer of cream and use a spatula to smooth it as much as you can. Top with the grated lime zest, cover the pan with plastic wrap or aluminum foil, and refrigerate for at least 8 hours or preferably overnight.

Crush the reserved cookies, sprinkle over the top of the cake, and serve. Cover any leftovers with plastic wrap and store in the fridge for up to 4 days.

BUÑUELOS

I grew up with buñuelos, crispy dough fritters that are flattened before frying and then sprinkled with cinnamon sugar while hot. We always had them around Christmas growing up, but Santi and I love them so much we make them all year long—pure nostalgia. Some people add egg or other ingredients to the dough, but since I love a double-duty recipe, I use my flour tortilla dough here. All you do is fry the rolled-out discs in oil instead of cooking them on the comal.

SERVES 8

Dough from Flour Tortillas
  (page 244)

All-purpose flour, for rolling out

½ cup granulated sugar

1 teaspoon ground cinnamon
  (preferably Ceylon/canela)

Good-quality olive oil (not
  extra-virgin), for deep-frying

Make the tortilla dough as directed and divide it into 8 equal portions. Roll into balls, cover with a clean kitchen towel, and rest for 15 to 20 minutes.

Line a baking sheet with parchment paper. Lightly flour a work surface and gently flatten one ball of dough with your hand. Using a rolling pin, start in the center of the dough and roll straight up one time, then straight down one time, then turn 90 degrees. Continue rolling, rolling, and turning until you achieve an even round about 6 inches across and ⅛-inch thick. Place the rolled tortilla on the lined baking sheet and cover with a kitchen towel to keep from drying out. Continue with the remaining dough.

In a large shallow bowl, combine the sugar and cinnamon. Line a sheet pan with paper towels and set a wire rack over the pan. Set both near the stove.

Pour ½ inch oil into a large deep sauté pan or medium Dutch oven (make sure it is wide enough to hold the buñuelos) and heat over medium heat to 350°F on an instant-read thermometer.

When the oil is hot but not smoking (if you dip the end of a wooden spoon into the oil and it immediately starts to bubble, it's ready), working with one buñuelo at a time, add a dough round to the hot oil and cook, gently pressing down with tongs or a wooden spoon to try and keep it submerged in the

(continued on next page)

oil. Once it is firm enough to flip and just starting to brown on the bottom, about 1 minute, gently turn it over and fry on the other side for another minute or so, again pressing down to try to submerge it in the oil, until the underside is golden. When lightly golden on both sides, transfer to the wire rack. Immediately sprinkle with cinnamon sugar, flipping the buñuelo with tongs to sugar both sides (this is important!).

Continue frying and sprinkling and serve immediately.

PASTEL DE ELOTE

Where savory meets sweet is my sweet spot, and pastel de elote, also called pan de elote, is a perfect example. It's no wonder this moist, almost custard-like dessert—which is like a mix between corn bread, cake, and corn pudding—is a Mexican staple. Most people credit Veracruz (and inland in Puebla) as this dessert's original birthplace, but you can find it all over Mexico. Because much of the corn used throughout Mexico is much starchier and less sweet than the corn we get in the US, many versions of this recipe don't call for any flour. Since I'm using fresh sweet corn, I add a mix of all-purpose flour and masa harina (the same type I use for the Sopes on page 138 and Gorditas on page 145) to get the right texture and flavor. This cake is lovely plain, but I especially like it with a scoop of vanilla ice cream.

SERVES 12

Softened unsalted butter, for the pan

¾ cup cake flour

¼ cup masa harina

1½ teaspoons baking powder

1 teaspoon kosher salt

4 large eggs

1 (14-ounce) can sweetened condensed milk

3 cups fresh corn kernels (from about 3 ears of corn)

1 stick (4 ounces) unsalted butter, melted and slightly cooled

Vanilla ice cream, for serving (optional)

Preheat the oven to 350°F. Line a 9-inch round cake pan with a round of parchment paper and grease generously with butter.

In a large bowl, whisk together the cake flour, masa harina, baking powder, and salt.

In a high-powered blender, combine the eggs, sweetened condensed milk, and corn and blend until combined but not totally smooth, 15 to 20 seconds.

Pour the corn mixture into the dry ingredients and whisk until just smooth, being careful not to overmix. Use a spatula to fold in the melted butter until combined. Pour the batter into the prepared pan, using the spatula to smooth out the top.

Bake until the top is golden brown and a toothpick comes out clean (or with just a crumb or two attached), 40 to 50 minutes.

Let cool in the pan on a wire rack for 15 minutes. Turn out onto the rack, peel off the parchment round, then invert it onto a serving plate or platter with the top of the cake facing up.

Serve with a scoop of ice cream if you like. Store any leftovers in an airtight container in the fridge for up to 3 days.

CHOCOFLAN

To be honest, I've never been a huge fan of flan, but chocoflan is a different story! This cake is like a magic trick—as it bakes, the layers swap, leaving you with a luscious flan that has risen to the top and the moistest chocolate cake ever on the bottom. Some of my cake batter often mixes in with the top layer of flan, but those clear separate layers when I cut into it always blow my mind. Because I need texture and crunch on everything, I top the finished cake with chopped pecans, but feel free to swap them out for a different nut or skip them altogether.

SERVES 12

Softened unsalted butter, for the Bundt pan

¼ cup cajeta or any store-bought caramel sauce (gently heated if not pourable)

1⅓ cups all-purpose flour

1 cup sugar

⅓ cup Dutch-process cocoa powder, sifted

1½ teaspoons baking powder

1 teaspoon espresso powder (optional)

½ teaspoon kosher salt

1 cup whole milk

1 large egg

1 teaspoon vanilla extract (preferably Mexican)

½ cup vegetable oil

FLAN

1 (14-ounce) can sweetened condensed milk

1 (12-ounce) can evaporated milk

4 large eggs

1½ teaspoons vanilla extract (preferably Mexican)

¼ teaspoon kosher salt

Preheat the oven to 350°F. Generously grease a 12-cup Bundt pan with butter. Use a spatula to spread the caramel in an even layer in the bottom.

In a medium bowl, whisk together the flour, sugar, cocoa powder, baking powder, espresso powder (if using), and salt.

In another bowl, whisk together the milk, egg, vanilla, and vegetable oil. Add the wet ingredients to the dry and mix with a spatula until everything is evenly combined and the batter is smooth. Transfer the batter to the prepared Bundt pan and use a spatula to even out the top.

Make the flan: In a high-powered blender, combine the condensed milk, evaporated milk, eggs, vanilla extract, and salt and blend until smooth, about 1 minute. Use a ladle to carefully pour the flan mixture over the cake, gently tipping the ladle to disperse the flan, taking care not to disturb the cake layer too much (you may get some of the cake batter rising up into the flan but don't worry—it will still look beautiful when you flip it out!). Set the Bundt pan inside a roasting pan or other large baking dish with high sides that holds the pan comfortably. Cover the Bundt pan tightly with foil.

Bring a large kettle of water to a boil and carefully pour it into the roasting pan, letting the water rise about 1 inch up the sides of the Bundt. Carefully transfer the roasting pan to the oven and bake until the flan is firm, about 1 hour 30 minutes (if you remove the foil and carefully give the pan a shake, it

¼ cup cajeta or other store-bought caramel sauce

⅓ cup roughly chopped pecans, toasted if you like (see Toasting Nuts and Seeds, page 39)

won't jiggle) and a toothpick comes out mostly clean (this is a very moist cake so some batter may still cling to the toothpick).

Carefully remove the roasting pan from the oven and lift out the Bundt pan, letting any water drip off the bottom, then place on a wire rack to cool for 1 hour. Transfer to the fridge to chill for at least 1 hour and preferably overnight.

When you're ready to serve, run a table knife or offset spatula around the edges of the cake to try and help release it from the mold. Put a serving platter on top of the Bundt pan, then quickly invert it, letting the cake drop down onto the platter. Garnish with the caramel sauce and chopped pecans.

FLOURLESS CHOCOLATE-CHILE CAKE

 Chocolate and chile is a classic combination in Mexico, dating back to the Olmecs, Mayans, and Aztecs. Before the Spaniards came along and added milk and sugar, cacao was served as a bitter drink, often mixed with fresh chiles and sometimes a little honey to sweeten. This dense, rich (and gluten-free!) cake, with its hint of smoky spice, plays on all those lovely flavor combinations.

SERVES 12

Softened unsalted butter, for the pan

8 ounces semisweet chocolate, roughly chopped

1 stick (4 ounces) unsalted butter, cut into tablespoons

½ cup granulated sugar

¼ cup grated piloncillo or lightly packed light brown sugar

4 large eggs, at room temperature

⅓ cup Dutch-process cocoa powder

1 teaspoon ancho chile powder

½ teaspoon cayenne pepper

¼ teaspoon kosher salt

Flaky salt

Freshly whipped cream, for serving

Preheat the oven to 350°F. Line a 9-inch round cake pan with a round of parchment paper and grease with softened butter.

Set up a double boiler by filling a medium saucepan with 1 inch of water and bringing it to a simmer over medium heat. Set a large heatproof bowl on top (make sure the bottom doesn't touch the water) and reduce the heat to low to maintain a gentle simmer. Add the chocolate and butter to the bowl and stir often with a spatula until both are melted, 3 to 5 minutes.

Remove the bowl from the heat and add the granulated and brown sugars, whisking to combine—the sugar won't totally dissolve, and the mixture will look a bit grainy. Add the eggs, one at a time, whisking well after each addition.

Set a sieve over the chocolate mixture and sift in the cocoa powder, ancho powder, and cayenne. Whisk to combine, then stir in the kosher salt. Transfer the batter to the prepared pan and sprinkle generously with flaky salt.

Bake until the cake is cooked around the edges but not fully set in the center and a toothpick inserted in the center comes out with some moist crumbs, 25 to 30 minutes.

Let the cake rest in the pan on a wire rack for at least 30 minutes. Turn the cake out onto the cooling rack, peel off the parchment, then invert it onto a serving plate or platter.

Serve each slice with whipped cream.

Chocolate

Chocolate is another crop endemic to Mesoamerica. Everyone talks about Swiss chocolate and French chocolatiers, but the Olmecs of Southern Mexico (along with the Mayans and Aztecs) were consuming chocolate thousands of years before it ever made its way to Europe. For centuries—dating as far back as 450 BC—chocolate was served as a bitter drink (the Nahuatl word for chocolate, *xocolatl*, means "bitter drink" or "bitter water") and was associated with the gods.

The Aztecs believed that chocolate was a gift given to them by the god Quetzalcoatl and drank it both hot and cold, often transferring it from one vessel to another to make it frothy, believing that the chocolate was for the body and the foam was for the soul. They also used it as medicine to treat fever and cough and even as a form of currency. In Aztec culture, chocolate was more valuable than gold!

Cacao and corn remain the two most important crops in Mexican mythology and culture, but these days, about 70 percent of the world's cocoa beans come from the Ivory Coast, Ghana, Nigeria, and Cameroon, much of it grown on large commercial farms. Like most crops, chocolate benefits from a permaculture environment, where the cacao grows among other local trees like mango and citrus. When it is monocropped, as it is often farmed on these large, commercial plantations, it is not only more prone to disease but also loses its nuanced flavor. An easy way to help support responsible growing practices is by reading the labels when you buy bar chocolate—I always look for fair trade certified and support Latin American farmers whenever possible.

PALETAS *Two Ways*

You can get paletas on just about any street in Mexico and there's almost always a huge assortment of flavors to choose from—coconut, lime, dulce de leche, and so many more! My family's favorites are mango with chamoy (for me) and strawberry (for Santi) so that's what you'll usually find in my freezer. These make a fun and easy dessert, but they're also a refreshing snack for kids, sweetened mostly by the natural sugar in the fruit, with just a small amount of added sugar. Feel free to change up the fruits based on what's sweet and in season—you may just need to play around and find the right balance of fruit, acid, and sugar.

MANGO-CHAMOY PALETAS

SERVES 8

2 medium very ripe mangoes, roughly chopped (about 3½ cups)

⅓ cup sugar

2 tablespoons fresh lime juice

¼ cup chamoy (see Chamoy, at right) or to taste

In a high-powered blender, combine the mangoes, sugar, lime juice, and ⅓ cup filtered water and blend until smooth, about 1 minute.

Pour 1 to 1½ teaspoons of the chamoy into each of eight 4-ounce ice pop molds, trying to get it to drip down the sides of the mold as much as possible so it doesn't all go to the bottom. Fill the molds up about one-third of the way with the mango puree, drizzle in another teaspoon or so of chamoy, and top with the remaining mango puree, trying to divide it evenly among the molds. Add the pop sticks (if they aren't attached to the top) and transfer to the freezer until frozen solid, at least 6 hours and preferably overnight.

Chamoy

Chamoy is a salty, tangy, slightly sweet and slightly spicy sauce typically made from dried or pickled fruit, dried chiles, sugar, limes, and sometimes hibiscus. You can find bottles of it at most Latin grocers or you can order it online. I love pairing chamoy with sweet mango for paletas (see above), but it is also delicious drizzled over fresh fruit or veggies like watermelon, jicama, or cucumber!

STRAWBERRY PALETAS

SERVES 8

1 pound strawberries, hulled and halved if small/medium or quartered if large (about 3½ cups)

⅓ cup sugar

2 tablespoons fresh lemon juice

In a large bowl, toss the cut strawberries and sugar together and let macerate for 20 minutes, until the strawberries have released much of their liquid, making a sweet red syrup in the bowl.

Transfer the macerated berries and their juices to a high-powered blender and add the lemon juice and ⅓ cup filtered water. Blend until smooth, about 1 minute.

Divide the strawberry mixture among eight 4-ounce ice pop molds, set the cover on top, add the pop sticks (if they aren't attached to the top), and transfer to the freezer until frozen solid, for at least 6 hours and preferably overnight.

GRILLED MANGO
with No-Churn Coconut Ice Cream

The grilled mango painted with recado negro (a special Yucatán spice paste) and served with coconut ice cream that I ate at chef Roberto Solís's restaurant Huniik in Mérida is one of the best desserts I've ever had. I had to re-create it as soon as I got home. I can't get my hands on recado negro in LA, but this is still incredible without it. This recipe makes a lot of ice cream, but we never have a problem getting through it!

SERVES 6

2 cups heavy whipping cream

1 (11.25-ounce) can sweetened condensed coconut milk

¼ teaspoon coconut extract (optional)

¼ teaspoon kosher salt

3 large mangoes

1 tablespoon coconut oil, melted

In a stand mixer fitted with the whisk, whip the cream, condensed milk, coconut extract (if using), and salt on medium-low and increase to medium-high speed, until the mixture holds stiff peaks, about 3 minutes.

Transfer the cream mixture to a 9-inch loaf pan, or similar, then press a piece of wax or parchment paper onto the surface and cover with plastic wrap. Freeze for at least 6 hours and preferably overnight.

Heat a grill or grill pan over medium-high heat.

Slice a sliver off of the bottom of the mango, so you can easily hold it upright. Slicing top to bottom, slice parallel to the pit (trying not to hit it) and cut down each flat and wide side. Repeat with the other mangoes until you have 6 "cheeks." Cut a crosshatch pattern into the flesh (this will make them easier to eat) and brush each with coconut oil.

Place the mango cheeks flesh-side down on the grill and cook, rotating 90 degrees halfway through, until you have nice grill marks and the fruit is starting to soften, 3 to 4 minutes total.

Divide among plates, flesh-side up, and top each piece of mango with a large scoop of coconut ice cream. Serve immediately.

Freeze leftover ice cream in an airtight storage container (or leave it in the loaf pan with the wax or parchment paper and plastic wrap) for up to 2 weeks.

BEBIDAS

An Ode to My Friend Tequila (and Some Other Fun Drinks)

This just might be my favorite chapter because it has everything from coffee to tequila—and even coffee with tequila! I included some great nonalcoholic drinks, too, but for the most part, this collection of recipes is an ode to my dear friend, tequila. I've always been a tequila girl—this agave-based liquor plays well with just about any mixer, has no sugar, and never gives me a hangover—so I'm not surprised that it's now one of the fastest-growing spirits in the world.

When I founded my tequila company, Casa Del Sol, I discovered my calling as a home mixologist. I love playing around to see which ingredients and mixers will complement, rather than overpower, the subtle notes of different kinds of tequila. Ginger beer and a little lime juice pair so well with the hints of vanilla in a blanco, and the butterscotch and honey notes in a reposado are so beautiful with espresso and vanilla liqueur. I've done a lot of cocktail research over the years and, between my own experimentations and the tips and tricks I've picked up from friends and bartenders along the way, I've developed a repertoire of truly "top shelf" tequila cocktails—not to mention a few coffee drinks and some refreshing, fruity sips you'll also find here.

CHAMPURRADO

I love atole—the hot, sweet, somewhat thick masa-based drink typically served around holidays like Día de Los Muertos and Noche Buena. When I learned that there's also a chocolate version, I was like, sign me up! I think of champurrado as a cross between hot chocolate and eggnog—thick, rich, and subtly spiced. I make this for Santi often and always serve it with tamales at Christmas (sometimes with a shot of tequila thrown in for good measure!).

SERVES 4

3 cups whole milk

1 Mexican chocolate tablet (I use Abuelita)

¼ cup grated piloncillo or lightly packed light brown sugar

1 teaspoon vanilla extract (preferably Mexican)

⅓ cup masa harina

In a medium saucepan, combine the milk, chocolate tablet, brown sugar, and vanilla. Bring the mixture to a simmer over medium-low heat and cook gently, stirring with a molinillo (placing it between your palms and vigorously rolling it back and forth) or whisk to make sure nothing is sticking, until the chocolate and sugar have dissolved, 5 to 8 minutes.

In a small bowl, combine the masa harina and 1½ cups water and whisk to make sure they are thoroughly combined. Slowly stir the masa mixture into the hot chocolate. Bring the mixture to a low boil, then reduce the heat and simmer gently for another minute, stirring with your molinillo or whisk to create some foam, until the drink is nice and thick.

Divide into mugs and serve.

CAFÉ DE OLLA

I've been enjoying the aroma of coffee since I was about six years old, when my mom first tasked me with making my dad's morning coffee—though it wasn't until I got to college and found myself suddenly cramming for midterms and finals that I started drinking it myself. But even as a child, I found the smell intoxicating. Café de olla is a very classic way to prepare coffee—simmered with cinnamon and star anise and sweetened with piloncillo—and is mostly found in rural areas and cooler climates in Mexico. *Olla* means "cooking pot" in Spanish, and traditionally this drink was prepared in an earthen clay pot, also used to cook beans and other drinks like Champurrado (page 204).

MAKES ABOUT 6 CUPS

½ cup grated piloncillo or lightly packed light brown sugar

1 cinnamon stick (preferably Ceylon/canela)

3 whole cloves

1 star anise

5 tablespoons coarsely ground dark roast coffee beans (don't use instant)

Fill an olla de varo or large saucepan with 6 cups water. Add the brown sugar, cinnamon stick, cloves, and star anise. Bring the mixture to a boil, then reduce to a gentle simmer and cook, stirring often, until the sugar has fully dissolved, 10 to 15 minutes.

Add the ground coffee and give it a good stir. Turn off the heat, cover, and let infuse for 5 minutes.

Pour through a fine mesh sieve and serve hot, alone or with steamed or regular milk if desired. Any leftovers can be stored in an airtight container in the fridge for a couple of days and either reheated in a small saucepan or turned into a delicious iced coffee!

AGUA DE PEPINO

 This cucumber water is ubiquitous in Mexico, where we drink it like lemonade. You'll be offered it in households, restaurants, bars, and by street vendors. I'll never say no to an agua de pepino—it always makes me feel like I'm at a spa, even when I'm sitting on a street corner scarfing down tacos.

MAKES ABOUT 3 QUARTS

2 medium slicing cucumbers or 1 large English cucumber

6 tablespoons granulated sugar

⅓ cup fresh lime juice (from 3 to 4 limes)

6 cups cold filtered water

Ice

Cucumber wheels, for garnish (optional)

Remove the peel from the cucumbers in strips, keeping some unpeeled (I like it for color), and then cut the cucumbers into chunks (you should have about 4 cups). Add the cucumber, sugar, lime juice, and 3 cups of the filtered water to a high-powered blender. Blend until smooth, about 2 minutes.

Pour the mixture through a fine-mesh sieve, pressing down to make sure you get all the juice. Transfer to a large pitcher and mix with the remaining 3 cups of filtered water. Store in the fridge for up to 2 days, being sure to give it a good stir before serving.

Serve over ice with cucumber wheels as garnish, if desired.

AGUA DE JAMAICA

 Agua de Jamaica (pronounced ha-mai-kah) got its name because the hibiscus flower, which gives this drink its signature magenta hue, was originally brought over to Mexico from Jamaica. We always have a jug of this in our fridge. I love how hydrating and refreshing it is, not to mention its gorgeous color! I prefer mine a little less sweet than you'll find in much of Mexico, but feel free to play around with the sugar and ratio of concentrated hibiscus syrup to water to make your perfect version. You'll usually see this served cold as an agua fresca, but I also love mixing the concentrate with hot water to make tea.

MAKES ABOUT 1 QUART
CONCENTRATE (ENOUGH
FOR 2 QUARTS AGUA
FRESCA OR HOT TEA)

6 tablespoons granulated sugar

1 cup dried hibiscus flowers
    (see Típ)

Cold sparkling or still water

Ice

In a large saucepan, bring 4 cups water to a boil. Add the sugar and stir to dissolve. Stir in the hibiscus flowers, cook for 5 minutes or until the flowers have started to cook down and the water is a beautiful pink color, then turn off the heat, cover, and steep for 15 to 20 minutes, until the water is a deep shade of magenta. Strain the concentrate and store in the refrigerator for up to 1 week.

For a full batch or a single agua fresca, mix the concentrate with equal parts cold sparkling or still water. Serve over ice. You can refrigerate agua fresca for up to 1 week.

TÍP: Dried hibiscus flowers
can be found at Latin markets
or online. If shopping in
person, look for dried flowers
that are still a little soft and
aren't faded or discolored.

CLASSIC MARGARITA

When I started my tequila company, Casa Del Sol, an amazing mixologist schooled me on what a classic margarita should be: tequila, agave, and lime. Nothing else. When you start with a good tequila, adding anything like Cointreau, simple syrup, orange juice, or a salt rim will just detract from the nuanced flavors of the spirit. The key to an amazing margarita is having amazing tequila. Keep that in mind, and it's hard to go wrong.

MAKES 1 MARGARITA

2 ounces (¼ cup) tequila blanco (or reposado or añejo; see Típ)

1 to 1½ ounces (2 to 3 tablespoons) fresh lime juice, depending how lime-y you like it

½ ounce (1 tablespoon) agave nectar

Ice

Lime wedge, for garnish

TÍP: Blanco is the tequila most often used for margaritas, but feel free to play around with different añejos and reposados for this (and any of the margarita recipes). I especially love my Casa Del Sol reposado, which has lots of vanilla notes, in this classic margarita.

Add the tequila, lime juice, and agave to a cocktail shaker filled with ice. Cover and shake vigorously for 10 seconds, until the drink is ice cold and frothy. Strain into a rocks glass with ice and garnish with a wedge of lime.

> ## Eva's Classic Margarita Dos and Don'ts
>
> NO salt on the rim. It distracts from the flavor of the tequila.
>
> NO orange liqueurs.
>
> NEVER use lime concentrate.
>
> And NO, you cannot use simple syrup! Only agave nectar, which comes from the same plant used to make tequila.

FLAMIN' HOT MARGARITA

The only thing better than a classic margarita is a spicy margarita! And this one is tops. I usually use jalapeño slices here, but serrano would also work well—just use less because they're usually spicier! Depending on what kind of strainer you have, the little seeds from the chiles might sneak into your drink. I don't mind (they add a little extra kick) but if you want to avoid them, be sure to use a very fine-mesh strainer. Don't skip the Tajín rim, which adds a little brightness, salt, and spice to every sip.

MAKES 1 SPICY MARGARITA

1 tablespoon Tajín, or as needed

1 lime wedge

2 thin slices jalapeño

1 to 1½ ounces (2 to 3 tablespoons) fresh lime juice, depending how lime-y you like it

½ ounce (1 tablespoon) agave nectar

2 ounces (¼ cup) tequila blanco

Ice

Spread the Tajín out on a small plate. Run the lime wedge around the rim of a rocks glass, coating it with lime juice. Dip and twist in the Tajín to make a spicy rim.

Combine the jalapeño, lime juice, and agave in a cocktail shaker and use a muddler or the end of a rolling pin to crush the chile slices up a bit.

Add the tequila and ice, cover, and shake vigorously for 10 seconds, until the drink is ice cold and frothy. Add fresh ice to the rimmed rocks glass and strain in the margarita.

The Amazing Agave Plant

We often associate agave with tequila and mezcal, but the plant has ties to Mexican religion, culture, and economics that far predate distillation. Its strong fibers have been turned into textiles and rope for thousands of years and, in pre-Columbian Mexico, its thorns were used as needles, and its sap, which has natural antiseptic and antimicrobial properties, was used as medicine. Agave sap was also fermented and turned into pulque—a sacred alcoholic drink for the Aztecs. It was ritually drunk by priests and warriors, offered to gods, and given to sacrificial people before ceremonies . . . because of its sanctified nature, most people were allowed to consume it only on special occasions—you could even be put to death if you were caught drunk from pulque in public!

The first mezcal (which is essentially a distilled version of pulque) is said to have been made in Oaxaca around 1565. Legend goes that when the Spanish conquistadors ran out of their precious brandy, rudimentary mud stills were constructed to make alcohol from the local agave plant. Though the Spanish may have introduced the technique of distilling agave, it was the Mexicans who mastered it, first in the form of mezcal and then tequila. The word *mezcal*—which comes from the Nahuatl *mezcali* and means

"oven-cooked agave"—refers to any agave-based spirit. So while all tequila is mezcal, not all mezcal is tequila. Like France's Champagne, there are very strict rules when it comes to what can be called tequila. This spirit can only be made from the blue Weber agave in the state of Jalisco or some limited municipalities in the states of Tamaulipas, Guanajuato, Michoacán, and Nayarit. Any agave-based spirit made from a different variety of plant or produced outside of these approved regions must be called "mezcal" or "agave spirit."

Traditional mezcal (and tequila!) making is a beautiful art form, one that is usually passed down from generation to generation in families who grow and harvest agave. Once the agave plants are dug up, their leaves are removed to reveal the heart or piña, which is then roasted in old-fashioned earthen pits or brick ovens called hornos (this is where many mezcals get their smoky flavor) to release its natural sugars. Next, the roasted piñas are crushed, often with the help of horses and a large stone wheel called a tahona, and left to ferment. The fermented juice is then distilled and either bottled (for blanco tequila or joven mezcal, for example) or put into barrels and aged into reposado, añejo, or extra añejo.

MEXICAN MULE

I'm a huge fan of ginger beer, but I've never liked vodka, so I always avoided Moscow Mules. Then I discovered the Mexican Mule, where you swap in tequila for the vodka—it's so much better! My compadre (and Santi's godfather) Amaury Nolasco taught me that the key to a great Mexican Mule is adding just a squeeze of lime. Unlike a margarita, where the lime is a major flavor component, here it should play a supporting role, balancing things out with just a touch of acid.

MAKES 1 MULE

Ice

2 ounces (¼ cup) tequila blanco

½ ounce (1 tablespoon) fresh
   lime juice

¾ cup ginger beer

1 lime wedge, for garnish

Fill a copper mug or highball glass with ice. Add the tequila, lime juice, and ginger beer. Stir with a straw and garnish with the lime wedge.

FRESH FRUIT MARGARITA

 Adding fresh fruit is another fun way to shake up the classic margarita. My go-tos are strawberry, blueberry, or watermelon (which is especially good with a Tajín rim), but any fresh ripe fruit works well. Just muddle the fruit with the lime juice and agave, add tequila, shake, and drink! I often do a dirty pour (when you pour directly from the shaker, ice and all, without straining), because I like the bits of muddled fruit in my glass. But you can also strain and garnish with a few whole or sliced pieces of fruit.

MAKES 1 FRUITY MARGARITA

¼ cup fresh fruit, left whole if small (like blueberries and raspberries) or chopped if large

1 to 1½ ounces (2 to 3 tablespoons) fresh lime juice, depending how lime-y you like it

½ ounce (1 tablespoon) agave nectar

2 ounces (¼ cup) tequila blanco

Ice

Whole or sliced fresh fruit, for garnish

Combine the fresh fruit, lime juice, and agave in a cocktail shaker and use a muddler or the end of a rolling pin to crush up the fruit.

Add the tequila and ice, cover, and shake vigorously for 10 seconds, until the drink is ice cold and frothy. Pour the whole mixture into a glass or strain into a rocks glass with ice, garnish with a small piece of fresh fruit, and serve.

MEXICAN HOTTY TODDY

My dad always told me that tequila cures everything, so every time I got a cough or a cold (as an adult, of course!), he'd tell me to take a shot of tequila. One day when I was making a lemon and honey concoction for my sore throat, I decided to go ahead and follow his advice and add a shot to my tea. Turns out he was right—it really does cure everything (and it did!). I make this when I'm a little under the weather but also as a cozy nightcap in the cooler winter months.

MAKES 1 HOTTY TODDY

2 ounces (¼ cup) tequila añejo

1 ounce (2 tablespoons) agave nectar

1 ounce (2 tablespoons) fresh lemon juice

¾ cup boiling water

Lemon wheel, for garnish

Add the tequila, agave, and lemon juice to a mug. Top with the boiling water, stir to combine, and garnish with a lemon wheel.

REPOSADO ESPRESSO MARTINI

I knew I would love this drink before I even tried it. Two of my favorite things in the world combined in one cocktail?! Yes, please! Many espresso martini recipes blend vodka and a coffee liqueur to add sweetness and balance, but when you start with a good reposado—which often has notes of caramel and a smooth, Cognac-like finish—you don't want to overpower it. I opt for a little vanilla liqueur instead, which allows the perfect pairing of pure tequila and coffee to shine through. If you can't find a vanilla liqueur, you can of course sub with Kahlúa or another coffee-based liqueur—never let an incomplete bar cart get in the way of a good happy hour or after-dinner drink!

MAKES 1 MARTINI

2 ounces (¼ cup) tequila reposado

1 ounce (2 tablespoons) freshly brewed espresso, cooled

1 ounce (2 tablespoons) vanilla liqueur, such as Xanath by the Gaya family or Drillaud

Ice

3 espresso beans, for garnish

Place a martini glass in the freezer to chill.

Combine the tequila, espresso, and vanilla liqueur in a cocktail shaker with ice. Cover and shake vigorously for 5 seconds, until icy cold and frothy. Strain into the chilled martini glass. Garnish with the espresso beans and drink immediately.

APEROL SPRITZ MARGARITA

This drink is like the love child of two of my favorite cocktails—an Aperol spritz and a margarita—and I can't believe I didn't discover it sooner! You get the sweetness from the Aperol and agave, the boozy punch from the tequila, and the brightness from the lemon juice, all topped off with sparkling water (instead of the traditional prosecco), making this feel like the most refreshing adult soda in the world. I can't get enough of them. I'm making it my life's mission to turn this into the drink of next summer.

MAKES 1 BUBBLY MARGARITA

Ice

2 ounces (¼ cup) tequila blanco

1 ounce (2 tablespoons) Aperol

1 ounce (2 tablespoons) fresh lemon juice

½ ounce (1 tablespoon) agave nectar

½ cup sparkling water, such as Topo Chico, or more to taste

Lemon twist, for garnish

Fill a large wine glass or highball glass with ice. Add the tequila, Aperol, lemon juice, and agave and stir to combine. Top with the sparkling water. Garnish with a lemon twist and enjoy!

BASICS THAT AREN'T BASIC

Lo Esencial

Mexican food isn't Mexican food without the "basics," like fresh salsas, pickled onions, and homemade totopos. These easy recipes, which may be called basic but are actually anything but, are my secret weapons for transforming nearly any dish from fine to fantastic. A drizzle of Tomatillo Salsa (page 234) gives a fresh, spicy bite to Grilled Spiced Shrimp Tacos (page 111) and a spoonful of crunchy Salsa Macha (page 237) instantly upgrades the Corn and Green Chile Soup (page 58)—and really, just about any recipe in this book or any book for that matter— from delicious to outstanding. And once you make tortillas from scratch (they're so easy, I swear), you'll never go back. So do yourself a favor, set aside a little time, and knock out these essentials to have in your fridge and pantry. And if your family is anything like mine, you should probably go ahead and make a double batch.

GUACAMOLE

There's really no wrong way to make guacamole (unless you're adding something sacrilegious like mayonnaise or garlic or peas!), but this is my current go-to recipe. I love the chunky guacamole from my last cookbook, but this creamier version is perfect for spooning over tacos, scooping up with Totopos (page 248), or dipping Chicken Taquitos (page 121) into.

MAKES ABOUT 2 CUPS

3 medium firm-ripe avocados

¼ to ½ small white onion, minced

1½ tablespoons fresh lime juice

3 tablespoons finely chopped fresh cilantro

½ small jalapeño or serrano chile, finely diced (seeded if you want less heat)

Kosher salt

In a medium bowl, combine the avocados, onion, lime juice, cilantro, and chile. Mash the avocados with a fork until mostly smooth. Season to taste with salt and serve immediately or store in an airtight container in the fridge for up to 2 days.

CHIPOTLE SALSA *(Salsa Roja)*

I learned this and the Tomatillo Salsa (page 234) from my friend Claudia, a registered dietician who has a wonderful website called The Diplomacy Diet. When I first tasted her salsas, I wanted to drink them, they were that good!! This spicy chipotle one is simple to make but has wonderful depth of flavor from the charred tomatoes and smoky chipotles. I spoon this over Carne Asada Tacos (page 112), Pork and Red Chile Tamales (page 132), and everything in between. I always cook both this and my tomatillo salsa on the stove for 5 to 10 minutes after blending. It both mellows and deepens the flavors and gives the salsas a lovely dark color. If you prefer a fresher taste (or are short on time), feel free to skip this step.

MAKES ABOUT 2 CUPS

4 small or 3 medium plum tomatoes

1 medium white onion, quartered

2 garlic cloves, unpeeled

3 canned chipotle peppers in adobo sauce

½ cup hot water

Kosher salt

1 tablespoon extra-virgin olive oil

Heat a medium comal, cast-iron skillet, or nonstick skillet over medium-high heat. When hot, add the whole tomatoes, onion, and whole garlic cloves and cook, flipping with tongs as needed, until nicely charred all over, 8 to 10 minutes.

Peel the garlic cloves and transfer to a high-powered blender along with the tomatoes, onion, and chipotle peppers. Add the hot water and blend until smooth, 1 to 2 minutes. Season to taste with salt.

In a sauté pan, heat the olive oil over medium heat. Add the salsa and cook, stirring often, for 5 minutes, until it has thickened slightly and darkened in color. Let cool and then transfer to glass jars and store in the fridge for up to 2 weeks.

PICO DE GALLO

Another classic I couldn't leave out, this punchy, spicy salsa is great for topping eggs, tacos, or Molletes (page 28), or just for dipping your Totopos (page 248)!

MAKES ABOUT 2½ CUPS

3 large Roma tomatoes, finely diced

½ small white onion, finely diced

1 medium serrano chile, minced (seeded if you want less heat)

⅓ cup finely chopped fresh cilantro

1 tablespoon fresh lime juice

Kosher salt

In a medium bowl, combine the tomatoes, onion, serrano, cilantro, and lime juice. Season to taste with salt and serve immediately or store in the fridge for up to 3 days.

RAW AVOCADO
AND
TOMATILLO
SALSA,
PAGE 235

PICO DE GALLO,
PAGE 231

TOMATILLO
SALSA,
PAGE 234

CHIPOTLE
SALSA,
PAGE 230

TOMATILLO SALSA *(Salsa Verde)*

I always make sure we have at least two jars of this salsa in our fridge because Pepe puts it on everything. Seriously. If we're eating Chinese food, he's pouring it over his chow mein; Japanese, he's dipping his hand rolls into the salsa. The man cannot get enough, and neither will you!

MAKES ABOUT 2 CUPS

12 medium tomatillos, husked and rinsed

1 large white onion, quartered

2 medium serrano chiles (or more if you like it spicy!), stemmed and halved lengthwise

3 garlic cloves, unpeeled

1½ cups roughly chopped fresh cilantro (about 1 small bunch)

½ cup hot water

Kosher salt

1 tablespoon extra-virgin olive oil

Preheat the oven to 425°F. Line a baking sheet with parchment.

Place the whole tomatillos, onion, serrano chiles, and garlic cloves on the lined baking sheet. Roast until the vegetables are charred and the tomatillos are starting to burst, 15 to 20 minutes. If you want a little more color, move the baking sheet to the upper third of the oven and broil on high for 3 to 5 minutes at the end.

Peel the garlic and transfer everything to a high-powered blender. Add the cilantro and hot water and blend until smooth, 1 to 2 minutes. Season to taste with salt.

In a sauté pan, heat the olive oil over medium heat. Add the salsa and cook, stirring often, until it has thickened slightly and turned dark green, 7 to 10 minutes. Let cool and then transfer to glass jars and store in the fridge for up to 2 weeks.

RAW AVOCADO AND TOMATILLO SALSA

 You were planning to put guacamole on your tacos anyway, so why not just mix it with your salsa? I love to serve this bright yet creamy salsa plain with Totopos (page 248), but it also adds welcome zest and texture to any taco or egg dish.

MAKES ABOUT 1½ CUPS

4 medium tomatillos, husked and rinsed

1 medium serrano chile (seeded if you want less heat)

1 tablespoon fresh lime juice

1 small garlic clove, finely chopped

¼ cup loosely packed roughly chopped fresh cilantro

1 medium avocado, diced

2 tablespoons finely chopped white onion (about ⅛ small onion)

Kosher salt

In a food processor, combine the tomatillos, serrano, lime juice, and garlic and blend until smooth, about 1 minute.

Add the cilantro, avocado, and onion and blend for another 10 seconds or so, just to mix and roughly chop—but not puree—everything. You want the texture to be chunky and rough.

Season to taste with salt and serve immediately or refrigerate in an airtight container for up to 1 week.

SALSA MACHA

This is Mexico's version of Asian chili crisp (and I think it's even better!). I discovered salsa macha on a trip to Valle de Bravo, a lakeside town just outside of Mexico City, where I bought a jar from a woman who was selling it on the street. Once I tried it, I couldn't live without it, but the salsa macha you can find at grocery stores in the States just doesn't compare. My version—with crispy garlic chips, gently fried dried chiles, and a lovely mix of crunchy seeds—is so good I could eat it straight from the jar . . . but I usually save it to spoon over avocado toast, eggs, soup, or anything that could use a little spicy crunch!

MAKES ABOUT 1½ CUPS

1¼ cups good-quality olive oil (not extra-virgin)

6 large garlic cloves, carefully peeled (not smashed first) and thinly sliced

3 dried guajillo chiles, stemmed and seeded

1 dried ancho chile, stemmed and seeded

2 dried árbol chiles, stemmed and seeded

3 tablespoons pumpkin seeds

2 tablespoons sunflower seeds

2 tablespoons sesame seeds

1 teaspoon apple cider vinegar

½ teaspoon granulated sugar (optional)

1 teaspoon kosher salt

Line a large plate with paper towels and set near the stove. In a small saucepan, combine the oil and garlic slices (leave the heat off). Give the pan a shake to make sure all the garlic slices are submerged in oil, then turn the heat to medium and cook, letting the garlic gently sizzle and reducing the heat as needed if they sizzle too much, until the garlic chips are golden but not at all burnt, 5 to 7 minutes. Use a slotted spoon to transfer all the chips to the paper towels (be sure to get every piece out of the oil otherwise they will burn and make your oil acrid).

Add the guajillo chiles to the oil and cook, pressing down with your slotted spoon to submerge them, until they become fragrant and lighter in color, about 1 minute. Transfer to the plate with the garlic chips to cool. Add the ancho and árbol chiles and cook for about 15 seconds, just until they bubble, and the ancho gets a little crispy. Transfer to the plate.

Add the pumpkin and sunflower seeds and cook, stirring to make sure they cook evenly, until golden, about 1 minute. Stir in the sesame seeds, turn off the heat, and let sit for 1 minute to lightly toast. Transfer the oil and seed mixture to a heatproof bowl and stir in the vinegar, sugar (if using), and salt.

Transfer the chiles to a cutting board, finely chop, and add to the oil.

Once the salsa has cooled completely, stir in the garlic chips, cover, and transfer to a covered glass jar or airtight container. Refrigerate for up to 3 weeks.

PICKLED RED ONIONS

This is another condiment I learned about in Mexico, although pickled red onions are popular in many cuisines throughout the world. In my recipe—inspired by the ones I ate up and down the Yucatán Peninsula—the onions are infused with a simple mix of vinegar, bay leaf, Mexican oregano, and black peppercorns. It's tangy and subtly sweet, and adds so much dimension and texture to any dish that could use a little brightness and punch. Which is nearly everything, right?

MAKES ABOUT 2 CUPS

1 small red onion, halved and thinly sliced

½ cup distilled white vinegar or apple cider vinegar

1 dried bay leaf

2 teaspoons kosher salt

1 teaspoon dried Mexican oregano

1 teaspoon sugar

½ teaspoon black peppercorns

Place the onion in a heatproof medium bowl.

In a medium saucepan, combine the vinegar, bay leaf, kosher salt, oregano, sugar, peppercorns, and ½ cup water. Bring to a simmer over medium heat and cook, stirring to help dissolve the salt and sugar, for 1 minute.

Pour the hot liquid over the sliced onion, cover with a clean kitchen towel, and let cool to room temperature. Transfer to an airtight jar and refrigerate for up to 2 weeks.

BACONY BORRACHO BEANS

I've been making a version of these beans practically my whole life, but the method has changed a bit over the years. When I became a mom, you better believe I pulled out the slow cooker! We go through these at an alarming rate in my house, so I needed a recipe that was quick to throw together and utterly foolproof. This is that recipe. Now, I throw everything in a slow cooker, cover with water, and wake up to the most flavorful, tender beans imaginable. And because the measurements are so easy to remember (3 cups beans, 3 tablespoons onion powder, 3 tablespoons garlic powder, etc.), I can make them in my sleep or easily ask my mom to put them on if I'm out. To make these vegan, just skip the bacon and use veggie bouillon cubes instead of chicken.

MAKES ABOUT 3 QUARTS

3 cups dried pinto beans

1 (10-ounce) can Ro-Tel diced tomatoes and green chiles

3 tablespoons onion powder

3 tablespoons garlic powder

3 chicken or vegetable bouillon cubes

1 (8-ounce) package bacon (optional but highly encouraged), slices tied together with twine

Kosher salt

In a slow cooker, combine the pinto beans, diced tomatoes, onion powder, garlic powder, bouillon cubes, and bacon strips. Cover with 12 cups water and season generously with kosher salt (I put in about 1½ tablespoons).

Cook on high for 10 hours, or until the beans are super tender and flavorful. Remove the bacon strips from the beans and serve immediately, turn into Refried Borracho Beans (page 242), or cool and refrigerate in an airtight container for up to 4 days.

REFRIED BORRACHO BEANS

I eat these refried beans with fresh flour tortillas for breakfast almost every morning, and they're the base for so many recipes in the book, like Enfrijoladas (page 37), Molletes (page 28), and Refried Bean and Jalapeño Tamales (page 137). I love the extra pork flavor I get from cooking in bacon fat (I have a little ceramic pig that I store my leftover bacon grease in), but a good Spanish olive oil is also delicious. I give exact amounts for fat and bean liquid here, but the truth is I always change it up depending on my mood, what I'm using them for, and how full my little piggy is. Whether you make them with lots of fat or just a little, runny or thick, these refried beans are above and beyond anything you could ever buy in a can.

MAKES ABOUT 2 CUPS

2 cups drained Bacony Borracho Beans (page 241) plus 2 tablespoons of their cooking liquid

1 tablespoon bacon fat or extra-virgin olive oil

In a food processor, combine the beans and the cooking liquid and blend, scraping down the sides with a spatula halfway through, until smooth, about 1 minute.

In a large sauté pan, heat the fat over medium heat. Add the beans and cook, stirring often, until thick and bubbling, about 5 minutes. Turn off the heat and serve.

FLOUR TORTILLAS

Flour tortillas will always be nostalgic for me because I learned to make them from my aunts back in Texas. I remember so clearly rolling out the dough, doing my best to make a perfect round, then cooking them on a hot comal until blistered on both sides. I'd eat them hot out of the pan, sometimes burning my fingers because I just couldn't wait. Now it's my morning tradition with Santi. He loves to help me measure the ingredients and roll out the dough. We both end up covered in flour and our tortillas often look more like the state of Florida than a perfect circle, but I wouldn't trade this tradition for the world.

MAKES TWELVE 6-INCH TORTILLAS

- 2 cups all-purpose flour, plus more for rolling
- 2 teaspoons kosher salt
- 2 teaspoons baking powder
- ¼ cup Crisco butter-flavored shortening, unsalted butter at room temperature, or extra-virgin olive oil
- ⅔ cup warm water, plus more as needed

To make the dough by hand, in a large bowl, combine the flour, salt, and baking powder. Add the shortening or other fat and use your fingers to mix until crumbly. Pour in the warm water, mixing it in with your hands. Add more warm water (about 1 tablespoon at a time) as needed until you have a rough ball, then knead for 2 to 3 minutes, until a smooth ball forms.

To make the dough in a food processor, quickly pulse together the flour, salt, and baking powder, just to combine. Add the fat and pulse until crumbly. With the motor running, slowly pour in the warm water, adding more as needed (1 tablespoon at a time), until a ball forms, then turn off the machine. The dough should now be ready to shape.

Divide the dough into 12 equal portions (or more or fewer depending on how big you want your tortillas) and roll into balls. Cover with a clean kitchen towel and rest for 15 to 20 minutes.

Line a baking sheet with parchment paper. Lightly flour a work surface and gently flatten one ball of dough with your hand. Using a rolling pin, start in the center of the dough and roll straight up one time, then straight down one time, then turn 90 degrees. Continue rolling, rolling, and turning until you achieve an even round about 7½ inches across and ⅛ inch thick. Place the rolled tortilla on the lined baking sheet and cover with a kitchen towel to keep from drying out. Continue with the remaining dough.

TIP: If you're going to eat only a few tortillas, roll them up into 12 balls but only roll out and cook what you're planning to eat. Store the remaining balls in an airtight container (I often use a zip-seal bag) in the fridge for up to 2 days so you can roll them out and cook them fresh as needed.

Heat a comal, cast-iron, or other nonstick skillet over medium heat. When the pan is hot, add the tortillas, one at a time, and cook until browned in spots on the bottom and you notice a few bubbles on the top, about 1 minute. Flip and cook for another minute or so, until there are brown spots on the other side.

Transfer to a tortilla warmer or wrap in a clean kitchen towel while you cook the remaining tortillas. Eat immediately or store any leftovers in an airtight container (I often use a zip-seal bag) in the fridge and reheat on a comal.

CORN TORTILLAS

It's no secret that I'm a flour tortilla girl and, no matter how many times Pepe tries to convince me otherwise, I'll always choose them over corn in the great tortilla debate. But I will concede that a good corn tortilla has its place. The recipe is simple, but to achieve a truly delicious corn tortilla, it is essential to start with masa harina made from nixtamalized corn (see Nixtamalization, page 136). I also highly recommend a tortilla press, because, as I learned while filming the show *Searching for Mexico*, rolling them out into perfect rounds takes a lot of practice!

MAKES TWELVE 5-INCH TORTILLAS

2 cups masa harina

1 teaspoon kosher salt

1½ cups warm water

In a medium bowl, combine the masa and salt. Add the warm water and mix with your hands until all the water is incorporated.

Divide the masa dough into 12 equal portions, roll into balls, and cover with a damp clean kitchen towel to keep from drying out.

Heat a comal or cast-iron skillet over medium-high heat. Line the bottom of a tortilla press with a piece of plastic (a zip-seal bag or produce bag works well) cut into a long rectangle so it covers the bottom of the press and can be folded over the masa ball to cover the top of the press, too. Place a ball of dough between the two layers of plastic and in the center of the press, and press down to flatten the dough into a 5-inch tortilla ¹⁄₁₆ inch thick. If you don't have a tortilla press, place the dough between the two sheets of plastic and press down with a heavy sauté pan or baking sheet, trying to exert even pressure so the tortilla is of an even thickness.

Carefully transfer the tortilla from the plastic liner to the palm of your hand, then place on the hot comal. Cook the tortillas, one at a time, for about 1 minute per side, until they are cooked through, possibly slightly puffed, and very lightly browned in spots.

Transfer to a tortilla warmer or wrap in a clean kitchen towel while you cook the remaining tortillas.

TOTOPOS

I love making my own tortilla chips! They're so much more delicious than anything you can buy at the store. And the recipe couldn't be simpler—it's just cut-up corn tortillas fried quickly in hot oil. These will level up your chilaquiles and make your guacamole and salsas taste a million times better. Of course, you can always buy a bag of tortilla chips, but give this recipe a try first and thank me later.

MAKES 6 OR 7 CUPS

Good-quality olive oil (not extra-virgin), for shallow-frying

12 corn tortillas, homemade (page 247) or store-bought, each cut into 8 wedges

Kosher salt

Line a baking sheet with paper towels and set a wire rack on top. Set near the stove. Pour ⅓ inch oil into a large deep sauté pan or Dutch oven and set over medium heat and heat until the oil is hot but not smoking (if you dip the end of a wooden spoon into the oil and it immediately starts to bubble, it's ready).

Add about one-third of the tortilla wedges (you want them to just fit in an even layer) and fry, moving them constantly with a wooden spoon or slotted spatula to try to get them to cook evenly, until very lightly browned, 2 to 3 minutes. Carefully remove with a slotted spoon or slotted spatula, place on the wire rack, and season immediately with salt. Repeat, in batches, with the remaining tortilla pieces.

Serve immediately or store in an airtight container at room temperature for up to 1 week.

TOSTADAS

I hate grocery store tostadas. They're often stale, and by the time I get them home, half the bag is usually broken. After too many ruined dinners, I started to make my own. Not only are homemade tostadas crunchy, fresh, and intact every time, but when you fry them in good olive oil, they also get infused with really great flavor. With a homemade tostada, the tostadas and ceviches on pages 92 to 102 taste extra special.

MAKES 8 TOSTADAS

Good-quality olive oil (not extra-virgin), for shallow-frying

8 (5-inch) corn tortillas, homemade (page 247) or store-bought

Kosher salt

Line a baking sheet with paper towels and set a wire rack on top. Set near the stove. Pour ½ inch oil into a large deep sauté pan or Dutch oven and heat over medium heat until the oil reaches 350°F and is hot but not smoking (if you dip the end of a wooden spoon into the oil and it immediately starts to bubble, it's ready).

Add a tortilla and fry, pressing down with tongs to try to keep it submerged in the oil, until just firm and lightly golden, 30 seconds to 1 minute. Use the tongs to carefully flip and cook on the second side, pressing down, until lightly golden, another 30 seconds to 1 minute.

Remove to the wire rack and sprinkle with a little salt. Repeat with the remaining tortillas.

Serve immediately or store in an airtight container at room temperature for up to 1 week.

ACKNOWLEDGMENTS

First and foremost, I want to thank everyone—the skilled guides, chefs, home cooks, farmers, and artisans—I met while filming the show *Searching for Mexico*. Thank you for guiding me, welcoming me into your restaurants, home kitchens, farms, and sacred spaces, and sharing your recipes and stories with me. This book would not exist without you:

In Mexico City, Gabriela Renterí, Ricardo Barroso, Alexis Alaya, Gabriela Cámara, Eduardo "Lalo" García, Anais Martinez, Luci (the queen of tlacoyos), Gabriela Hernández Chalte, everyone at Casa Tochan, and Edo López.

In the Yucatán, Luis Ronzón; Roberto Solís; Don Enrique; Alberto Kuku and his mother, Casimira; Regina Escalante; Don Pepe and Maria; and Miriam Azcorra.

In Nuevo Léon, Alejandro Gutiérrez and family; Jero Alvarado and Neto Esquivel; Doña Mary; Katya Schoening; Hugo Guajardo; Jorge Montemayor; Doña Lupita; Cindy and Louisa; Ana Rodriguez and her mother, Marta; Aturo and Fede Salazar; and Rodrigo, Patricio, and Daniel Rodrigo Rio.

In Oaxaca, Alex Ruiz; Omar Alonso; Janet López Canseco and her father, Juan; Celia Floriàn; my Muxe friends on the Isthmus of Tehuantepec; Amado Ramírez Leyva; Ponciano Méndez Galván and family; Sylvia Philion; Doña Berta; and Thalía Barrios García.

In Jalisco, Wendy Perez, Óscar Segundo and Xrysw Ruelas Diaz, Jesús Moro, Enrique Gonzalez Villareal, Fabian Delgado Padilla, Rocío Moreno, Vicente, and all the Coca people, Alejandra Pelayo and Mariana Padilla, and Salvador Rosales Trejo.

In Veracruz, Erik Guerrero, Ana de la Reguera, Itzel Mendoza, Nidia Hernández Medel, Norma Gaya and family, Doña Marta and all the Smoke Women, and Luis Palmeros and Doña Rocío.

Thank you to my wonderful editor, Raquel Pelzel, designer Mia Johnson, art director Stephanie Huntwork, and the rest of the team at Clarkson Potter: Elaine Hennig, David Hawk, Felix Cruz, Stephanie Davis, Patricia Shaw, Alexandra Noya, and Kim Tyner.

A huge thank-you to the entire photography team for bringing the book to life with your beautiful, vibrant images: Matt Armendariz, Adam Pearson, Abby Pendergrast, Wade Hammond, Joe Elgar, Diana Kim, Elle Debell, and Kitty Rheault.

Lastly, to my family, especially my big and little chilangos, Pepe and Santi. You are my whole heart and my favorite people in the world to cook for.

INDEX